DEMCO

THE FRONTIER IN AMERICAN CULTURE

THE FRONTIER

THE NEWBERRY LIBRARY   CHICAGO

IN AMERICAN CULTURE)

An Exhibition at the Newberry Library, August 26, 1994–January 7, 1995

ESSAYS BY
RICHARD WHITE
PATRICIA NELSON LIMERICK

EDITED BY
JAMES R. GROSSMAN

UNIVERSITY OF CALIFORNIA PRESS   BERKELEY   LOS ANGELES   LONDON

University of California Press

Berkeley and Los Angeles, California

University of California Press, Ltd.

London, England

Library of Congress Cataloging-in-Publication Data
White, Richard, 1947–
    The frontier in American culture : an exhibition at the Newberry
  Library, August 26, 1994–January 7, 1995 / essays by Richard White
  and Patricia Nelson Limerick : edited by James R. Grossman.
      p. cm.
  Includes bibliographical references.
    ISBN 0-520-08843-3 (alk. paper). — ISBN 0-520-08844-1 (pbk. :
alk. paper)
    1. Frontier and pioneer life—West (U.S.)—Exhibitions. 2. West
(U.S.)—History—Exhibitions. 3. Turner, Frederick Jackson.
I. Limerick, Patricia Nelson, 1951– . II. Grossman, James R.
III. Newberry Library. IV. Title.
F596.W562 1994
978´.02´0747731—dc20   94-8534

Printed in the United States of America

9 8 7 6 5 4 3 2 1

The paper used in this publication meets the
minimum requirements of American National
Standard for Information Sciences—Permanence
of Paper for Printed Library Materials, ANSI
Z39.48–1984.

Designer: Steve Renick

Compositor: G&S Typesetters, Inc.

Text: 11.5/15.5 Bembo

Display: Copperplate Condensed

Printer/Binder: Data Reproductions Corp.

For Ann

Funding for this exhibition and catalogue has been provided by

The National Endowment for the Humanities

"Emigration to the Western Country,"
from Benson J. Lossing, *Our Country: A
Household History for All Readers from the
Discovery of America to the Present Time*
(New York, 1878), vol. 2.

CONTENTS

ACKNOWLEDGMENTS

As a historian who had neither published work related to the history of the frontier nor organized an exhibit, I came to this project in dire need of help. In the ensuing months, I was the beneficiary of more support than I had initially thought necessary and more than I could ever have expected to receive. I certainly never expected that as word of what we were doing spread, I would find on my desk a copy of a supermarket tabloid whose headline reinforced our idea of the frontier as a set of metaphors *anyone* could inhabit: "SPACE ALIENS HELPED INDIANS BEAT CUSTER." This and other, more prosaic, items that we accumulated during the long planning process enhanced my growing realization that the frontier is in fact a ubiquitous presence in American popular culture. Friends who shared my unfamiliarity with frontier historiography also shared this growing realization as they found that promises to "watch out for useful stuff" had them constantly clipping newspapers and noting what they were seeing in stores, catalogues, and elsewhere in their daily lives. Fortunately, we can now leave this activity to Patricia Limerick, whose essay in this volume suggests the extent to which we only scratched the surface.

The Newberry Library is a small institution by academic standards, with approximately one hundred employees complemented by a remarkably dedicated corps of volunteers. At one point or another virtually every member of the Newberry staff contributed energy and expertise to this project. I cannot overstate the continuing pleasure of working with such energetic, knowledgeable, and humane colleagues. In particular I would like to thank James Akerman, John Aubrey, Dick Bianchi, Richard Brown, Ken Cain, Laura Edwards, Emily Epstein, Fred Hoxie, Ruth Hamilton, Kathryn Johns, Robert Karrow, Harvey Markowitz, Patrick Milton, Joan ten Hoor, David Thackery, Carol Sue Whitehouse, Mary Wyly, and the entire paging staff of special collections.

During the three years of work on this project a number of colleagues have generously contributed time and expertise. Kathleen Neils Conzen, William Cronon, David Gutiérrez, Patricia Limerick, Martin Ridge, and Donald Worster constituted a genial but critically insightful advisory board during the planning stage. Among the countless scholars to whom we are grateful for suggestions, Sharon Boswell, Brian Dippie, Paul Fees, and Ramon Price were especially helpful in the identification and location of appropriate images. Karen Kohn's expertise in the winnowing of images and creation of a preliminary design brought two scholars with limited visual skills to the point where we actually could envision how all this might look in a gallery. The exhibit itself was designed by Kent Gay and Cliff Abrams, of Abrams, Teller, Madsen, Inc.

Planning and implementation grants from the National Endowment for the Humanities have been essential, and I am grateful to David Martz for his willingness to provide the kind of candid criticism that one needs to write a decent proposal. Funding has also been provided by AT&T. The Dr. Scholl Foundation has provided resources through its generous support of the Newberry's Dr. William M. Scholl Center for Family and Community History.

Most of the items in this exhibition are in the Newberry Library Collections. We have, however, either borrowed or reproduced materials from a number of institutions. We wish to thank the following for their generosity: Anheuser-Busch Corporate Archives, Buffalo Bill Historical Center, Chicago Historical Society, Robert L. Parkinson Library & Research Center at Circus World Museum, Remington Museum, C. M. Russell Museum, State Historical Society of Wisconsin, and Washington University Art Gallery.

This catalogue would not have been possible, at least not in this form, without the enthusiasm, persistence, and good sense of Eileen McWilliam of the University of California Press. I am also grateful to Richard White and Patricia Limerick for writing essays and to the anonymous readers enlisted by the Press for providing criticism and suggestions. Stephanie Fay brought everything together in the final stages, working patiently with a difficult manuscript.

Hilah Geer prepared the catalogue checklist. I had no idea how difficult that task would be; I'm not sure she did either. Nevertheless, she has done it with remarkable care, attention to detail, and good cheer. As registrar for the exhibition she has also been indispensable to its fruition.

This is Richard White's exhibition. Its ideas are his ideas; its insights reflect his scholarship. Richard's patience, energy, good humor, and generosity have contributed mightily to the pleasure I associate with this project. He has also served as a model colleague, teacher, and collaborator.

JAMES R. GROSSMAN

INTRODUCTION

The existence of an area
of free land, its continuous
recession, and the advance
of American settlement
westward, explain
American development.

Frederick Jackson Turner, 1893

The bullet
is the pioneer of
civilization, for it has
gone hand in hand with
the axe that cleared the forest, and
with the family Bible
and school book.

William F. Cody, 1893

COWBOYS, INDIANS, LOG CABINS, wagon trains. These and other images associated with stories about the frontier maintain a constant presence in our lives. Innumerable products are marketed according to assumptions that symbols of the frontier are deeply embedded in Americans' notions of who we are and what we want to be. "Somewhere along the line everybody wants to be a cowboy," intones the narrator of a radio advertisement for pickup trucks. Mounted in the fall of 1994 at the Newberry Library, "The Frontier in American Culture" explores our national preoccupation with frontier images, metaphors, stories, and reenactments.

In 1893 the Columbian Exposition brought to Chicago two men, each of whom told a story about the American frontier and the American West. "The Frontier in American Culture" is an exhibition about the stories told by this unlikely duo—a University of Wisconsin history professor, Frederick Jackson Turner, and the most flamboyant showman in late-nineteenth-century America, "Buffalo Bill" Cody. The stories differed in genre, tone, and content. Nevertheless, we have paired them here, just as they were paired in Chicago in 1893, because they invariably exist in relation to each other—whether separate or entangled.

Frederick Jackson Turner told—and subsequently published—a story presented in the form of historical scholarship. For all its later influence, relatively few people actually heard his Chicago paper, "The Significance of the Frontier in American History." This story of the peaceful settlement of "free" land, framed as a sweeping explanation of the evolution of a uniquely democratic, individualistic, and progressive American character, attained its initial influence among Turner's academic colleagues. Partly because of its resonance with existing images and stories, Turner's version of American history and character spread easily—through the classroom, through journalism, and through popular histories. The notion that the West was something we settled, rather than conquered, pervades

American storytelling and iconography; the contrast with the Spanish conquistadores has never been subtle either in popular culture or in elementary and secondary education texts.

Turner's story marginalized Indians, virtually dismissing them as merely a part of the wilderness environment. Buffalo Bill, on the other hand, presented to his much broader audience a narrative filled with Indians—warriors who had to be conquered if America was to fulfill its destiny. His "Wild West" extravaganzas reproduced classic "western" scenes, most of which entailed major roles for guns and large animals. A re-creation of the Battle of the Little Bighorn, "Custer's Last Stand," often stood at the center. Cody's dramatization, more accessible and more sensational than Turner's essay (which itself is strikingly readable compared with stereotypical academic prose), gained more immediate and direct influence. Thousands of Americans saw each performance of his Wild West extravaganza, which he never called a show because that would have suggested it was something less than a true story. It was, of course, much less—or more, considering Cody's capacity to invent and embellish. Whatever one's skepticism about scholarly objectivity and the implications of the historian's power to select the elements of a narrative, one cannot doubt that Cody's narrative was, in a sense, less "true" than Turner's. But it was equally, if not more, influential, and therefore sufficiently important historically to stand alongside Turner's essay.

"The Frontier in American Culture" juxtaposes these two powerful narratives of the frontier, narratives that agree on the fact of significance but not its content. A "story about stories," the exhibition explores how a belief in the significance of the frontier emerged as what the historian Warren Susman has described as "the official American ideology." As consumers, readers, or travelers, Americans are surrounded with, and surround themselves with, the frontier metaphors described in Patricia Limerick's essay in this volume. As an aspect of our collective consciousness, the frontier has become virtually irremovable. That "constructed" frontier, however, has been anything but immutable. Richard White's essay, like the exhibition itself, explains how diverse groups of Americans have asserted their legitimacy in American culture by clothing themselves (both literally and metaphorically) in frontier garb and revising frontier narratives to accommodate their histories. By presenting the creation, fate, and significance of frontier stories, the exhibition challenges its audience to think about the relation between history, popular culture, and national identity.

This relation underlies the evolution of the exhibition itself. "The Frontier in American Culture" was conceived originally as a commemoration (although not a celebration) of Turner's address at the Columbian Exposition. Working on the assumption that the Turner thesis itself exercises little continuing influence on modern scholarship, the Newberry in 1990 asked Richard White to develop an exhibition that would be "less a retrospective view than a prospective one." Indeed, White was among the scholars whose exciting new work on the American West self-consciously avoided both Turner and the idea of the frontier. But both Turner and retrospect were, in fact, inescapable. In the early 1990s a curious phenomenon was emerging in the national press—curious, at least, to a generation of "New Western Historians" who were suddenly a focus of attention in major newspapers and magazines and on radio. This remarkable media interest in "anti-Turnerian" scholars and their work owed to the "discovery" by journalists that the "frontier thesis" they had learned in school bore little relation to contemporary scholarship on the West.

The questions reporters asked, and the stories they wrote (and continue to write), assumed that Turner still occupied the center of an academic debate. Yet most academics had relegated him to the periphery years ago. Historians thus found themselves summoned by reporters to reargue a series of controversies they had assumed were as dead as Turner himself. The frontier thesis in the minds of reporters, and apparently their readers, remains vital; it persists as the standard explanation of western and American exceptionalism. It remains so deeply embedded in a wider constellation of images about the West and the United States that the reporters regarded any questioning of it as radical and daring.

Many professional historians reacted to the media stories with understandable bewilderment. How could recent criticism of Turner's frontier thesis serve as the basis for a new history when the thesis had possessed limited influence among academic historians for nearly half a century? What historians were forgetting was the vast gap between academic and popular notions of the past. To most Americans the Turnerian frontier (though few knew it was "Turnerian"), along with Buffalo Bill's Wild West, constituted our frontier heritage.

The deep significance many Americans attach to this heritage emerged even more dramatically in the controversy over "The West as America," a 1991 exhibition at the National Museum of American Art. Labels accompanying the familiar work of such artists as Frederic Remington informed viewers that what seemed simple depictions of western life and events were actually "ideological narratives." In a tone the museum director later admitted could have been "lighter," labels explicitly confronted the paintings, castigating the artists for their ideas about race, class, gender, and war. A record number of visitors passed through the galleries, generating a remarkable guest book. The comments, which ranged from accolades to the dismissal of the exhibition as "perverse," are striking for their extent and vehemence. Two United States senators (at least one of whom had not seen the show) voiced their outrage over the Smithsonian's complicity in debunking our frontier.

Like the media coverage of the New Western History, the controversy over "The West as America" exhibition highlighted the gap between scholarly trends and popular understandings of history. But rather than make this a cause for lamentation or the occasion for propagating a "correct" view, we decided to ask why this aspect of American history resonated among the public with such depth and emotion. As the essays in this volume demonstrate, the answer lies in the common concerns that underlie even the most contradictory frontier narratives. Americans continue to tell variants of these stories because they are as much about the American future as the American past. The legacy of the histories enacted in Turner's essay and on Cody's stage tell us not only who we were (and are) but how we got to be that way, and who among us gets to be included in the "we." "A settler pushes west and sings his song," asserted Ronald Reagan in his second inaugural, "that's our heritage, that's our song." It is "the American sound." Understanding the stories generated by the frontier and the symbols that constitute its song helps us to reflect on whether there is a single "American sound." Perhaps there are many American sounds, each (like Turner and Cody) at once compatible and in conflict with one another.

· · ·

"The Frontier in American Culture" is a library exhibition comprising mainly books, manuscripts, and other library materials. The heart of this exhibition draws substantially on two collections at the Newberry, the Everett D. Graff Collection of Western Americana and the Edward E. Ayer Collection (focusing on European exploration, pioneer experiences, and Native Americans). These might be described as quintessentially "Turnerian" collections: Turner's fascination with the West was a more sophisticated version of the preoccupations of collectors such as Ayer and Graff. Similarly, the growing interest of late-nineteenth- and early-twentieth-century midwesterners in the histories of their families and communities underlies the origins of the Newberry's extraordinary local and family history collection. Once gathered, collections like those at the Newberry shape our national stories by influencing what scholars see when they come to do research. Historians today come to the Newberry to write new stories, based on earlier collectors' notions of the significance of the frontier.

As a presentation primarily of library materials, therefore, "The Frontier in American Culture" suggests how library collections reflect trends in scholarship and popular culture while nurturing the evolution of each. Visitors not only see the variety and range of the Newberry collections in a particular subject area but also understand why such a collection exists, why and how it evokes particular sentiments, and how historians use it to construct narratives and explanations. While individual books, films, and other modes of communication generally tell a single story—even if a complex one—a library houses innumerable stories. Indeed, the urge to continue building a collection rests on the recognition that new perspectives are constantly emerging, raising new questions and laying frameworks for new stories.

RICHARD WHITE

FREDERICK JACKSON TURNER AND BUFFALO BILL

AMERICANS HAVE NEVER had much use for history, but we do like anniversaries. In 1893 Frederick Jackson Turner, who would become the most eminent historian of his generation, was in Chicago to deliver an academic paper at the historical congress convened in conjunction with the Columbian Exposition. The occasion for the exposition was a slightly belated celebration of the four hundredth anniversary of Columbus's arrival in the Western Hemisphere. The paper Turner presented was "The Significance of the Frontier in American History."[1]

Although public anniversaries often have educational pretensions, they are primarily popular entertainments; it is the combination of the popular and the educational that makes the figurative meeting of Buffalo Bill and Turner at the Columbian Exposition so suggestive. Chicago celebrated its own progress from frontier beginnings. While Turner gave his academic talk on the frontier, Buffalo Bill played, twice a day, "every day, rain or shine," at "63rd St—Opposite the World's Fair," before a covered grandstand that could hold eighteen thousand people.[2] Turner was an educator, an academic, but he had also achieved great popular success because of his mastery of popular frontier iconography. Buffalo Bill was a showman (though he never referred to his Wild West as a show) with educational pretensions. Characteristically, his program in 1893 bore the title *Buffalo Bill's Wild West and Congress of Rough Riders of the World* (Figure 1).[3] In one of the numerous endorsements reproduced in the program, a well-known midwestern journalist, Brick Pomeroy, proclaimed the exhibition a "Wild West Reality . . . a correct representation of life on the plains . . . brought to the East for the inspection and education of the public."[4]

Although Turner, along with the other historians, was invited, he did not attend the Wild West; nor was Buffalo Bill in the audience for Turner's lecture. Nonetheless, their convergence in Chicago was a happy coincidence for historians. The two master narrators of American westering

FIGURE 1. *Buffalo Bill's Wild West and Congress of Rough Riders of the World: Historical Sketches and Programme*, Chicago, 1893.

had come together at the greatest of American celebrations with compelling stories to tell. The juxtaposition of Turner and Buffalo Bill remains, as Richard Slotkin has fruitfully demonstrated in his *Gunfighter Nation,* a useful and revealing one for understanding America's frontier myth.[5] The Newberry exhibition juxtaposes Turner and Buffalo Bill for reasons somewhat different from Slotkin's. But like Slotkin the exhibition takes Buffalo Bill Cody as seriously as Frederick Jackson Turner. Cody produced a master narrative of the West as finished and culturally significant as Turner's own.

Turner and Buffalo Bill told separate stories; indeed, each contradicted the other in significant ways. Turner's history was one of free land, the essentially peaceful occupation of a largely empty continent, and the creation of a unique American identity. Cody's Wild West told of violent conquest, of wresting the continent from the American Indian peoples who occupied the land. Although fictional, Buffalo Bill's story claimed to represent a history, for like Turner, Buffalo Bill worked with real historical events and real historical figures.

These different stories demanded different lead characters: the true pioneer for Turner was the farmer; for Buffalo Bill, the scout. Turner's farmers were peaceful; they overcame a wilderness; Indians figured only peripherally in this story. In Cody's story Indians were vital. The scout, a man distinguished by his "knowledge of Indians' habits and language, familiar with the hunt, and trustworthy in the hour of extremest danger,"[6] took on meaning only because he overcame Indians. He was, as Richard Slotkin has emphasized, the man who ultimately defeated them.[7] In Turner's telling the tools of civilization were the axe and the plow; in Buffalo Bill's, the rifle and the bullet. The bullet, the Wild West program declared, was "the pioneer of civilization."[8]

As different as the two narratives were, they led to remarkably similar conclusions. Both declared the frontier over. Turner built his talk on "the closing of a great historic movement."[9] The opening paragraph of Buffalo Bill's 1893 program gave a conventional enough account of the "rapidly extending frontier" and the West as a scene of "wildness." But it concluded with a significant parenthetical addition: "This last [the existence of a wild, "rapidly extending frontier"], while perfectly true when written (1883), is at present inapplicable, so fast does law and order and progress pervade the Great West."[10] The frontier, which according to Buffalo Bill had opened on the Hudson, had now closed. Indeed, Buffalo Bill the Indian fighter and rancher had become Buffalo Bill the promoter of irrigated farming.[11]

Both Turner and Buffalo Bill credited the pioneers with creating a new and distinctive nation, and both worried about what the end of the frontier signified. Buffalo Bill reminded his audience that generations were settling down to enjoy "the homes their fathers located and fenced for them."[12] But by implication the pioneers' children who inherited the West were a lesser breed. The pioneers had disdained, in the Wild West program's metaphor, to crowd into cities to live like worms. But with the West won, with free land gone, urban wormdom seemed the inevitable destiny of most Americans.[13]

The major elements of Turner's and Cody's stories were not new in 1893. Take, for example, the close of the frontier. Predictions of the frontier's imminent demise had been current for a quarter of a century. In 1869 Albert Richardson's popular *Beyond the Mississippi* was predicting the end of an era:

> Twenty years ago, half our continent was an unknown land, and the
> Rocky Mountains were our Pillars of Hercules. Five years hence,
> the Orient will be our next door neighbor. We shall hold the
> world's granary, the world's treasury, the world's highway. But we
> shall have no West, no border, no Civilization, in line of battle,
> pressing back hostile savages, and conquering hostile nature.[14]

Theodore Roosevelt rather begrudgingly credited Turner with having "put into shape a good deal of thought that has been floating around rather loosely."[15] And numerous historians have found elements of the Turner thesis presaged in one form or another in the scholarship of the late nineteenth century.[16] Forty years ago Henry Nash Smith took the process one step further by making the Turner thesis itself an expression of the nineteenth-century pastoral myth of the garden.[17]

To contextualize Turner, and indeed Buffalo Bill, however, creates a mystery rather than solves one. For if these ideas and symbols were so prevalent, how did the particular versions offered by Turner and Buffalo Bill come to be so culturally dominant and persistent? Why did they over-shadow, and indeed erase, their antecedents and competitors? No one, after all, reads Richardson; and Pawnee Bill—sometimes Buffalo Bill's partner, sometimes his competitor—is known only to antiquarians.[18]

The answer has two elements. First, the very contradictions between Turner's story and Buffalo Bill's suggest a clue. Turner and Buffalo Bill, in effect, divided up the existing narratives of American frontier mythology. Each erased part of the larger, and more confusing and tangled, cultural story to deliver up a clean, dramatic, and compelling narrative. Richardson, for example, had offered a narrative of conquest that emphasized both hostile nature and hostile "savages." Turner took as his theme the conquest of nature; he considered savagery incidental. Buffalo Bill made the conquest of savages central; the conquest of nature was incidental. Yet both Turner's and Buffalo Bill's stories, it must be remembered, taught the same lessons. Second, the very ubiquity of frontier icons allowed both Turner and Buffalo Bill to deliver powerful messages with incredible econ-omy and resonance. Precisely because they could mobilize familiar sym-bols, Buffalo Bill in a performance of several hours and Frederick Jackson Turner in a short essay could persuade and convince their audiences.

Both Buffalo Bill and Turner were geniuses at using frontier iconogra-phy. They capitalized on our modern talent for the mimetic—our ability to create countless mass-produced imitations of an original. In putting their talents to use, they drew on existing stories as well as on symbols, from log cabins to stagecoaches, that were reproduced over and over in American life. Turner incorporated such icons into his talk; Buffalo Bill adapted them as stage props. Indeed, he re-created himself as a walking icon, at once real and make-believe. As the 1893 program put it at a time when Buffalo Bill was forty-seven years old, "Young, sturdy, a remarkable specimen of manly beauty, with the brain to conceive and the nerve to execute, Buffalo Bill par excellence is the exemplar of the strong and unique traits that characterize a true American frontiersman."[19]

Frederick Jackson Turner: Regression and Progress

Turner's "frontier thesis" quickly emerged as an incantation repeated in thousands of high school and college classrooms and textbooks: "The existence of an area of free land, its continuous recession, and the advance of American settlement westward explain American development."[20] Turner asserted that American westering produced a succession of frontiers from the Appalachians to the Pacific; the essence of the frontier thesis lay in his claim that in settling these frontiers, migrants had created a distinctively American democratic outlook. Americans (gendered as male) were practical, egalitarian, and democratic because the successive Wests of this country's formative years had provided the "free" land on which equality and democracy could flourish as integral aspects of progress. Turner's farmers conquered a wilderness and extended what Thomas Jefferson had called an empire of liberty.[21]

Turner summoned the frontier from the dim academic backcountry, but in popular American culture the frontier already stood squarely in the foreground. Turner did not have to tell Americans about the frontier; he could mobilize images they already knew. Ubiquitous representations of covered wagons and log cabins already contained latent narratives of expansion and progress. Americans had recognized for generations the cultural utility of the frontier in their politics, folklore, music, literature, art, and speech. All Turner had to do was to tell Americans about the SIGNIFICANCE of this familiar frontier.

Turner masterfully deployed the images of log cabins, wagon trains, and frontier farming—and the stories that went with them. He fashioned these into a sweeping explanation of the nation's past. Along with the familiar themes of conquering a "wilderness" and making homes upon the land, Turner emphasized another, less familiar, theme: in advancing the frontier, a diverse people of European origins had remade themselves into Americans. "The frontier," he declared, "is the line of most rapid and effective Americanization."[22] "In the crucible of the frontier the immigrants were Americanized, liberated, and fused into a mixed race, English in neither nationality nor characteristics."[23] Turner had extended the meaning of progress. Progress was not merely an increase in material well-being but was cultural as well: growing democracy, greater equality, more opportunity.

Like his academic peers, Turner used no visual images to illustrate either the talks he gave or the academic articles he wrote. Instead, he relied on an almost painterly prose that evoked familiar scenes of migration, primitive beginnings, and ultimate progress. Americans already thought in terms of great achievements from primitive beginnings; Americans already thought of themselves as egalitarian and democratic. They had already symbolized such beliefs in images of log cabins and migration into a land of opportunity, and had turned those images into icons. Turner used the icons.

Turner often placed himself and his audience not in the West but in popular representations of the West. He instructed his audience to "stand at Cumberland Gap and watch the procession of civilization marching single file—the buffalo following the trail to the salt springs, the Indian, the fur trader and hunter, the cattle-raiser, the pioneer farmer—and the frontier has passed by."[24] He asked them to stand figuratively where George Caleb Bingham placed the viewer in *Daniel Boone Escorting Settlers through the Cumberland Gap* (Figure 2).[25]

This figure standing at the gap, or on the height or border, and watching progress unfold was one of the central American icons of the frontier. Its elements were at once relatively constant and quite flexible. The observer might—as in the Bingham painting, or in Francis Palmer's 1866 lithograph *The Rocky Mountains—Emigrants Crossing the Plains,* or in the illustration "Emigration to the Western Country" (see Frontispiece)—face

FIGURE 2. George Caleb Bingham, *Daniel Boone Escorting Settlers through the Cumberland Gap.* Oil on canvas, 1851–52. Courtesy Washington University Gallery of Art, Saint Louis. Gift of Nathaniel Phillips, 1890.

the emigrant party already on the road. They are surrounded by a vast emptiness and, in Bingham's painting, darkness. A second variant placed the viewer on a height behind the migrants, who were now, more often than not, departing from the known and familiar and heading west, as in "The March of Destiny" (Figure 3). Indians might appear on the margins of the picture, but the space into which the migrants moved was to be understood as vast and devoid of people (see Plate 1).

The emblematic titles of such pictures as "The March of Destiny" made their meaning obvious. Such didacticism was a common device. In one of the most familiar pictures of westward movement, the Currier and Ives print *Across the Continent: "Westward the Course of Empire Takes Its Way"* (Figure 4), a wagon train wends westward in the distance, but it is almost incidental. A railroad train steaming toward the center of the picture now bears the major burden of progress. The train leaves two Indians literally in its smoke as it departs a frontier village on its way west, while in the distance two more Indians pursue a fleeing herd of buffalo.

Turner, in standing with his readers at Cumberland Gap or South Pass, invoked these representations of settlement as a movement of pioneers into a largely uninhabited nature. This was how the pioneers themselves understood their experience. Wagon trains, Indians quietly moving to the margins of the scene, and the steady progression into the open and available West were the symbols used, for example, in the 1890 commemorative pictorial map of the route of the Mormon pioneers (see Plate 2). It is no wonder that Turner's interpretation of the West evoked such a deep popular response. The Turnerian plot resonated with already-familiar images of westward migration.

Standing on the height and watching progress unfold was the dominant image of the Turnerian story, but its power rested on two other Turnerian ideas: that the "free land" into which the pioneers moved was available for the taking and that American progress began with a regenerative retreat to the primitive, followed by a recapitulation of the stages of civilization.[26] Turner gave these ideas a powerful, almost epigrammatic, formulation and

ACROSS THE CONTINENT.

FIGURE 3 (*opposite*). "The March of
Destiny," from Colonel Frank Triplett,
*Conquering the Wilderness; or, New Pictorial
History of the Heros and Heroines of
America* . . . (New York, 1883).

FIGURE 4 (*opposite, below*). *Across
the Continent: "Westward the Course of
Empire Takes Its Way,"* 1868.

argued that they explained all of American history. The iconography of
the frontier had already prepared his audience to accept these bold claims
as mere common sense.

By the nineteenth century western North America was represented
conventionally on maps as largely empty and unknown. But earlier maps,
those of the sixteenth and seventeenth centuries, for example, had portrayed a densely occupied continent teeming with people. The 1718 *Carte
de la Louisiane et du Cours du Mississipi* (Figure 5) depicted an occupied
continent with Indian as well as European towns and villages. A similar
1776 map of the region east of the Mississippi showed an equally inhabited
interior. Although Europeans had only a partial knowledge of this interior, they assumed that it was occupied.[27]

By the nineteenth century all this had changed. In illustrated maps, as in
contemporary prints depicting the progress of pioneers, only a few scat-
tered Indians appeared. They were either retreating or quietly observing
the coming of whites. The maps Americans studied at school broadcast
the same message even more forcefully. The map of the early republic in
the companion atlas to Emma Willard's widely used nineteenth-century
school text vividly portrays the West as empty land (Figure 6). Small villages of French Canadians appear on the map, but Willard has completely
erased Indians. This message of settlers peacefully occupying vacant territory recurred in the popular literature of the West. Joaquin Miller's "Westward Ho," for example, celebrated a conquest "without the guilt/Of studied battle."

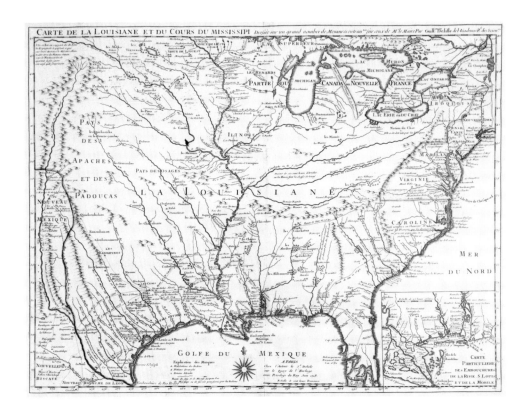

FIGURE 5.   Guillaume de Lisle, *Carte de la Louisiane et du Cours du Mississipi,* 1718.

> O bearded, stalwart, westmost men,
> So tower-like, so Gothic built!
> A kingdom won without the guilt
> Of studied battle, that hath been
> Your blood's inheritance. . . .[28]

Turner, like Miller, recognized conflict with the Indians, but for him it was merely part of a much larger contact with wilderness that engulfed settlers in a primitive world and necessitated the pioneers' initial regression

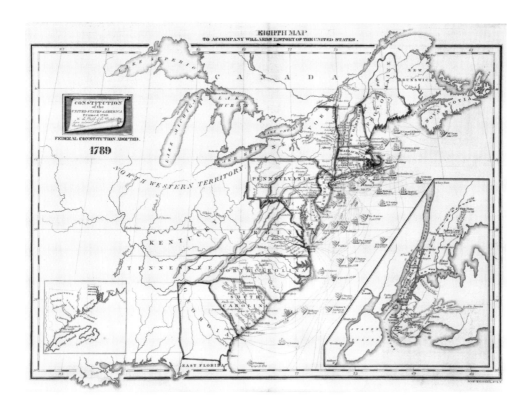

FIGURE 6.   Eighth map in the bound
series of maps that accompanies Emma
Willard's *History of the United States, or
Republic of America . . .* (New York, 1828).

and subsequent recapitulation of the stages of civilization. Conquest was
not "studied," it carried no burden of "guilt."

Turner symbolized the initial regression from which future progress
sprang with the log cabin. The "wilderness," he declared in Chicago,
"masters the colonist. . . . It puts him in the log cabin of the Cherokee and
Iroquois."[29] Through the log cabin, Turner linked pioneers with Indians
and wilderness. By the 1890s the log cabin had long been the chief icon of
the nineteenth-century frontier, if not of American culture itself. It marked
both regression, as the wilderness mastered the settler, and the beginning

An American Log-house.

FIGURE 7. "An American Log-house," from Georges Henri Victor Collot, *Voyage dans l'Amérique septentrionale . . .* (Paris, 1826).

of the recapitulation of civilized progress. A cabin, built with simple tools from local materials, proclaimed self-reliance and a connection with place. Usually isolated, it stressed the courage of the builder and the challenge that the surrounding wilderness represented. But most of all, the cabin had come to represent progress.

This link to progress was not intrinsic. Indeed an early representation of the log cabin, the etching in the atlas accompanying Georges Henri Victor Collot's *Voyage dans l'Amérique septentrionale,* only hints at progress (Figure 7). The woman standing at the door identifies this cabin as the home of a family rather than a hunter, and the stumps suggest the family's intention to farm. But the message of progress is diluted and ambiguous. The stumps, juxtaposed with the beautiful, haunting trees and the primitive and isolated structure, give no strong indication of change for the better. Even at mid-century the log cabin sometimes retained its tinge of rustic backwardness. George Caleb Bingham's painting of a squatter's cabin has little of the progressive about it.[30] And later, in different contexts, sharecroppers' cabins or cabins in Appalachia represented backwardness and poverty rather than progress and prosperity.

Only when coupled with a knowledge of the success to follow did the cabin proclaim great achievements from small beginnings. This was its purpose in William Henry Harrison's Log Cabin campaign and in the Lincoln presidential campaign. On the cover of the sheet music *Tippecanoe, the Hero of North Bend: Six Patriotic Ballads* (Figure 8), published in 1840, the portrait of Harrison looms like the sun over a log cabin, which basks in reflected glory. Presidential birth or residence in a log cabin assumed meaning only in light of the subsequent presidency.[31] The achievements of modern America made frontier cabins symbols of progress. The cabin demanded such pairings to evoke the historical narrative of national progress accomplished through self-reliance and individual energy.

Local and popular histories made similar use of cabin imagery. In Joseph Smith's *Old Redstone* (1854) a set of four illustrations (Figure 9) progressed from a "Log Cabin Meeting House" to "A Meeting House of 2nd Class" (still a log cabin) and finally to the ornate twin-towered "First Presbyterian

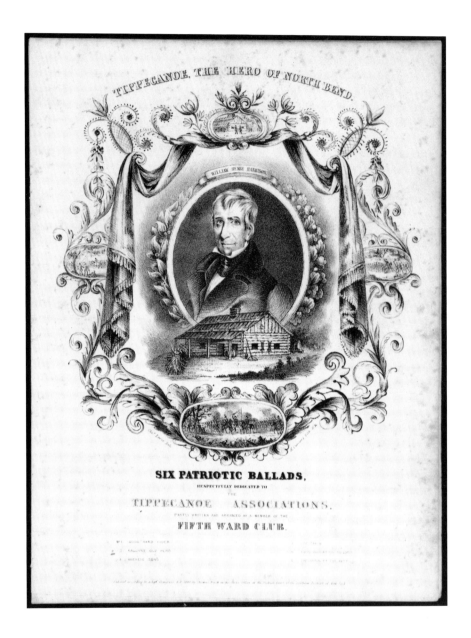

FIGURE 8. *Tippecanoe, the Hero of
North Bend: Six Patriotic Ballads . . .*
(New York, 1840).

FIGURE 9.   Illustration from Joseph Smith, *Old Redstone; or, Historical Sketches of Western Presbyterianism: Its Early Ministers, Its Perilous Times, and Its First Records.*

Church, Pittsburg, Pa." Such visual narratives provided a tangible groundwork for Turner.

But the cabin iconography that probably most clearly prefigured Turner appeared first in county atlases and then in the county histories that proliferated throughout the Midwest in the 1880s. These books commonly featured illustrations of prosperous contemporary farms that included, either in the picture itself or in an inset, a log cabin. The movement from the cabin to the developed farm signified progress. In many cases the message was made explicit. In the *History of Calhoun County, Michigan* (Figure 10), portraits of Ira A. Warren and Susan J. Warren framed an inset of a cabin, while the bottom half of the picture portrayed their current farm. In the *History of Ingham and Eaton Counties,* the large and lavish "Residence of Jas. T. Bullen" served as a symbol of his success, but hovering above it is an

FIGURE 10. Residence of Ira A. Warren, from H. B. Pierce, *History of Calhoun County, Michigan* (Philadelphia, 1877).

inset of a small cabin behind a split-rail fence labeled "First Home in the Woods."[32]

Images of personal progress could also illustrate collective progress. Early maps of Chicago employed the same progressive imagery as the county histories. A poster entitled *Chicago in Early Days, 1779–1857,* originally published in 1893, traces Chicago's development from fur-trading outpost and Indian town to growing city.[33] In the insets surrounding the map, cabins yield to frame buildings. A second poster published the same year, *Chicago in 1832* (Figure 11), focuses on a placid "faithful" view of the early settlement. But insets show both the city's geographical expansion by the 1890s and the extraordinary growth of its population.

FIGURE 11. George Davis, *Chicago
in 1832*. A later version (1893) of progressive imagery in Chicago maps.

Turner defined American culture as progressive, but the progress he en-
visioned was achieved, paradoxically, by retreating to the primitive along
successive frontiers. Being in "continuous touch with the simplicity of
primitive society" shaped American character.[34] New frontiers implied a
constant reinvigoration of the country and its people. "American development has exhibited not merely advance along a single line, but a return to
primitive conditions on a continually advancing frontier line, and a new
development for that area." Turner framed these ideas with an elegance
and sophistication beyond that of the writers and illustrators of county histories and popular accounts of pioneer life. But he adopted the theme of
these works, which had, in effect, prepared the way for him. Midwestern

farmers who understood their own lives as tracing the trajectory of progress from log cabins to prosperous farms, or Chicagoans not far removed from the time when their city was an Indian town with only a fur trader's cabin representing non-Indian occupation, formed an ideal audience for Turner. His themes would resonate with readers because he gave sophisticated form to what they already believed. His story of the country mimicked and validated their stories of their own lives and collective accomplishments. Their story became the American story.

The inhabitants of the various American Wests, no matter what their actual descent, considered their lives American. The environment of the frontier made them so. They said as much in the county histories and in the biographical dictionaries, or mugbooks, that followed them. In popular histories as well, the frontier acted like an acid eating away the immigrants' past and forcing them to remake themselves in the present as representative Americans. James W. Steele in *The Sons of the Border* (1873) declared:

> The Borderer is a man not born, but unconsciously to himself, *made* by his surroundings and necessities. He may have been born on the Chesapeake or the banks of Juniata; he may hail from Lincolnshire or Cork: far Western life will clothe him with a new individuality, make him forget the tastes and habits of early life, and transform him into one of that restless horde of cosmopolites who form the crest of the slow wave of humanity which year by year creeps toward the setting sun.[35]

In basing the genuine American character upon the experience of pioneers—an experience that at once stripped them of their past and gave them a new and uniform set of American characteristics—Turner conceptualized what was already conventional.[36] With the frontier as an organizing idea, he built a monumental narrative whose framework would guide the study of American history in succeeding generations.

Buffalo Bill told another story and deployed a different set of icons. His narrative differs most noticeably from Turner's in the roles assigned to Indians (Figure 12). On Turner's frontier Indians were not so much absent as peripheral; they were not essential to the meaning of his narrative. But Indians were everywhere in Buffalo Bill's Wild West. Illustrations of Indians were prominent not only in advertisements but throughout the program. A "horde of war-painted Arapahoes, Cheyenne, and Sioux Indians" participated in the Wild West.[37]

The role of these Indians in the show was to attack whites. Many of the great set pieces of the Wild West—"A Prairie Emigrant Train Crossing the Plains," the "Capture of the Deadwood Mail Coach by the Indians," and, the most famous of all, "The Battle of the Little Big Horn, Showing with Historical Accuracy the Scene of Custer's Last Charge"—featured Indian attacks.[38]

Buffalo Bill offered what to a modern historian seems an odd story of conquest: everything is inverted. His spectacles presented an account of Indian aggression and white defense; of Indian killers and white victims; of, in effect, badly abused conquerors. Such reenactments open a window onto a particularly interesting aspect of American iconography of the frontier. To achieve Joaquin Miller's "kingdom won without the guilt/Of studied battle," Americans had to transform conquerors into victims. The great military icons of American westward expansion are not victories, they are defeats: the Alamo and the Battle of the Little Bighorn. We, these stories say, do not plan our conquests—we do not, in Joaquin Miller's words, fight "studied battles." We just retaliate against barbaric massacres.

Like Turner, Buffalo Bill found both the theme and the icons for his narrative readily available. The theme of white victimization was so common that Turner himself, in what amounted to an aside, also made conquerors into victims. He spoke of Indians as a "common danger" that kept alive "the power of resistance to aggression." He, as much as Buffalo Bill, presented this striking reversal of the actual history as mere conventional

FIGURE 12. "Sitting Bull and Buffalo Bill." Postcard (no date).

wisdom.[39] Popular iconography gave this reversal of roles its power, sur-rounding Americans with images of valiant white victims overpowered by savage assailants. In the version of the frontier Buffalo Bill developed, the continent was no longer empty; it teemed with murderous Indian enemies.

Buffalo Bill exploited an iconography that stretched back to Puritan captivity narratives and continued through the wars of the eighteenth and early nineteenth centuries. Along with captivity narratives and popular fiction, nineteenth-century accounts of assaults by the Indians, such as the "Massacre of Baldwin's Family by the Savages" and "Murder of the whole Family of Samuel Wells . . . by the Indians" (Figure 13), kept this theme of white victimization central to the American understanding of Indian wars. Pictures of Indians attacking helpless white women and children or badly outnumbered white men became a staple of nineteenth-century popular histories (Figure 14).[40]

Indeed, the theme of Indian aggression persisted even after the United States had placed the Indians on reservations. As Buffalo Bill restaged the Little Bighorn in Chicago, the *Chicago Tribune* carried accounts of Indian aggression and white defense, with headlines in June and July 1893 pro-claiming "Fears of Outbreak . . . Agent's House Is Surrounded and He Is Compelled to Send for Aid," and "Maddened by Liquor: Indians at Leech Lake Threaten to Do Serious Harm," and, finally, "Indians Attempt to Lynch a Farmer."[41]

Buffalo Bill played no small part in making the image of Custer's defeat and the slaughter of most of his command the chief icon of this theme of the conquering victim.[42] Where representation stopped and lived experi-ence began were never very clear in Buffalo Bill's Wild West, especially with regard to Buffalo Bill's relationship to Custer (Figure 15). This ambi-guity gave the Wild West its power. Buffalo Bill created what now seems a postmodern West in which performance and history were hopelessly in-tertwined. The story Buffalo Bill told gained credence from his claim (and the claim of many of the Indians who accompanied him) that he had lived part of it.

The show and lived historical reality constantly imitated each other. Sit-ting Bull, whom Americans credited with being the architect of Custer's

MURDER of the whole family of Samuel Wells, cons[isting of himself, wife,] sister and eleven children, by the Ind[ians.]

Extract of a letter from a gentleman in New Orleans, to his friend in New-York, dated May 1, 1809.

"DEAR SIR,

I HAVE this day received information of one of the most aggravating murders that can be found recorded in history, perpetrated by the savages a few weeks since, in the interior parts of the country—the particulars of which are as follows :—The family of a Mr. Samuel Wells, who have resided somewhere about two hundred miles up the river Missouri, was on the night of the 10th of April last awakened from their slumber by the hideous yells of savages near the door of their dwelling—the family of Mr. Wells consisting of himself, wife, and eleven children, the youngest an infant—Mr. Wells on learning the cause of the disturbance arose and after securing the doors, furnished his family with such weapons as could be procured, himself and five eldest sons with each a musket, and his wife and sister and eldest daughter with an' ax each ; thus equipt did they wait for the attack of their unmerciful foes !—the Indians finding their doors secured, began to cut and hew them in pieces with their tomahawks, having succeeded in demolishing one, ten or twelve of them frightfully painted and with uplifted tomahawks rushed in !—here now commenced a scene horrid beyond conception : Mr. W. and his sons after having discharged their pieces with the best effect, with clubbed muskets attacked their savage foes, while Mrs. Wells her sister and her daughter were as busily employed with their fatal weapons. Sharp was the bloody fight and such the foe.

Their similar force returned them blow for blow ;
By turns successfully their force defy'd
And conquest wav'ring seem'd from side to side.

—In a few moments did this valiant little band succeed in clearing their house of their savage enemies, of those who entered nine lay lifeless on floor ; the remainder of the Indians now retiring for a few moments, afforded Mr. Wells and his sons an opportunity to reload, and once more secure the passage made by them ; in about half an hour the Indians (exasperated at their loss) returned and renewed their attack with redoubled fury, and with increased bravery did the unfortunate family repel the attack ! every door and window being doubly guarded, death was the sure portion of him that entered ! the floor was literally strewed with dead bodies of the savages, who were at length partially foiled by the assailed.—For nearly three hours did this bloody contest continue, when alas ! a fatal accident, the assailants gave up in their hellish object ! Mr. Wells and his sons having broken their muskets and rendered them unserviceable, the former dispatched one of the latter for a kettle of ax & hatchet which had been left in the barn, flattering himself that his son would be able to obtain them without hazarding his safety, by ascending a ladder in the floor of the house and unperceived by the savages reach the barn—but, alas, he was no more to return to his miserable parents ! the assailants after the falling, in their attempts at overpowering the unfortunate family had dispatched one of their gang to fire the barn, which he was in the act of doing when the lad entered ; discovering his danger he attempted to escape by flight but was pursued by the Indian, overtaken, and thrust into the barn, which was at that instant in a blaze, amidst the shrieks of the un-

fortunate youth, were too much to be withstood by the distracted mother ! in a fit of despair she broke from the arms of her husband & with an uplifted axe fled to the assistance of her wretched child ! but alas, the feeble efforts of the poor woman, were unavailing ! surrounded by the blood thirsty foes she was compelled to yield to their superior force !

The remainder of the family being thrown into confusion and the doors left unguarded, they became an easy prey to the unmerciful savages, by whom they were all made prisoners and bound severally with cords—the savages next proceeded to plunder the house of its most valuable effects, after which they set it on fire !

The miserable captives were now hurried into an adjoining thicket, where those infernal bloodhounds commenced their tragical work !—six saplings having been stripped of their branches, their tops were bent to the ground, to the ends of which each of the unfortunate captives (Mr. Wells excepted) were bound ; the sapling being then permitted with great rapidity forced along with them and extended in the air the unfortunate victims, the adjacent groves in the mean time resounding with their lamentations and entreaties for mercy ; alas, a scene like this could not fail to affect the heart of any but barbarians !

The savages were now commanded by their leader to try their skill in the dexterous use of their tomahawks ; the unhappy victims suspended between heaven and earth were the objects to which they were to be aimed ! Alas, O heavens ! how unspeakable must have been the feelings of the unhappy father at this moment ! bound hand and foot, he was compelled to stand an eye witness to the sufferings of his tor-

tured family ; the inf[ants] now flew thick around [the] limb were detached f[rom the] bodies ! and not until t[he] tinct, was the bloody t[omahawk laid] to close the tragic scen[e] *These vile of warfare a[—]* *By undistinguish'd plu[nder]* *They torture man and be[ast in]* *rage,*
Nor tender infant spare[s.]

Fortunately for Mr. [Wells the sav]ages intended for more [tor]ture) they discovered a m[—] keg of rum, of which be[ing fond] they drank to excess, a[nd] of intoxication suffered [—] Mr. Wells fled to the n[—] related to the afores[aid] particulars of the trag[edy—] the number of twenty [—] diately in pursuit of the [savages] serving as a guide. T[he] extract of a letter from [—] was one of the party.

Great was the rage a[nd venge]ance which every hear[t—] every countenance exp[—] to the place where th[e] some to the adjacent ri[ver] in hopes of vengeance [—] pointed. The bodies [of the] family were found co[vered] from the wounds mad[e] and scalping knife. [Moth]er with her infant & [—] shoulders, one of its li[ttle] hair ; their spirits wer[e—] who gave them ; the o[—] breathed, but her eye [—] quick followed. I f[—] next day when they [—] must have moved a h[—] side each other were t[—]

FIGURE 13. "Murder of the whole Family of Samuel Wells, consisting of his wife and sister and eleven children, by the Indians: Extract of a letter from a gentleman in New Orleans, to his friend in New-York, dated May 1, 1809."

HEROISM OF A PIONEER WOMAN.

" In the meantime his heroic wife was busily engaged in defending the door against the efforts of the only remaining Indian, whom she so severely wounded with the ax, that he was soon glad to retire."

defeat, toured afterward with the Wild West. And a famous picture (reproduced in Figure 12) shows him, in a long eagle-feather headdress, posing with Buffalo Bill before a studio backdrop.[43] Some of the Sioux who charged Custer at the Little Bighorn would later charge him nightly in the Wild West. Indians who fought whites in Cody's Wild West would return to the Dakotas to fight whites for real during the culmination of the Ghost Dance troubles that led to the slaughter of the Sioux at Wounded Knee in 1890. Buffalo Bill would step off the stage during both the Custer Campaign and the Ghost Dance to serve as an army scout, each time incorporating aspects of his experience into the show.[44]

FIGURE 14 (*opposite*). "Heroism of a
Pioneer Woman," from Henry Howe,
*The Great West: The Vast, Illimitable,
Changing West* (New York, 1860). Not all
women were portrayed as helpless victims.

FIGURE 15 (*above*). "Custer's Last
Fight." Poster advertisement, first edition.
Anheuser-Busch Brewing Association,
St. Louis, Mo., 1896. Photograph cour-
tesy of the Anheuser-Busch Corporate
Archives, St. Louis.

The most dramatic and revealing example of this complicated mimesis is the Yellow Hand incident. Leaving the stage in Wilmington, Delaware, in June 1876, Buffalo Bill had joined the Fifth Cavalry as a scout. He was in the field when the Sioux defeated Custer. During a skirmish that July, he had killed and scalped the Cheyenne Hay-o-wei, whose name was translated Yellow Hand (see Plate 3).[45] The skirmish with Yellow Hand, a piece of reality staged as theater, was being assimilated into Buffalo Bill's stage persona even as it happened. Buffalo Bill had prepared for the anticipated engagement by dressing in his showman's costume—"a Mexican vaquero outfit of black velvet slashed with scarlet and trimmed with silver buttons and lace"—which in his performances became the very clothing in which he had fought Yellow Hand.[46]

Killed by a man in theatrical dress, Yellow Hand died only to have Buffalo Bill resurrect him for the stage melodrama entitled "The Red Right Hand; or the First Scalp for Custer."[47] Buffalo Bill dispatched Yellow Hand nightly, repeatedly taking that "first scalp." Meanwhile Yellow Hand's actual scalp went on display in theaters where Buffalo Bill performed in what the program described as another "realistic Western Drama," *Life on the Border* (Figure 16). Yellow Hand had become a prop that validated Buffalo Bill's stories.[48]

Buffalo Bill, particularly in his identification with Custer, provided what Turner left out: the story of the conquest of the Indians. He did it by adopting a mythic mode already familiar to Americans, that of heroic victims and their rescuers and avengers (see Plate 4). The posters for Buffalo Bill's Wild West showed Indian assaults on covered wagons, Indian assaults on the Deadwood stage, and Indian assaults on small beleaguered bands of white men who valiantly defended themselves against circling warriors (see Plate 5). On the rare occasions when whites attacked, they were clearly coming to the rescue. In one scene Buffalo Bill and his Rough Riders charged in to save a white man being burned at a slow fire, a weeping white woman on her knees beside him (see Figure 24).[49]

Whereas Turner called forth well-known images in words, Buffalo Bill literally brought images to life. Where books, paintings, and some other shows depicting Indians offered only words, pictures, or white actors, Buffalo Bill presented actual Indians, who now inhabited their own representations. This was the most complicated kind of mimesis. Indians were imitating imitations of themselves. They reenacted white versions of events in which some of them had actually participated. In a way that prefigured the movies, Buffalo Bill enacted history. For millions of people his representation of the West became the reality. The genius of Buffalo Bill was to recognize the power of the mimetic, of the imitation, in the modern world.

Captain Jack Crawford, who joined Buffalo Bill in these pre–Wild West performances in 1877, was equally attuned to the power of the mimetic. Captain Jack, the Poet Scout (Figure 17), went on to a long career of his own, but Custer and Buffalo Bill gave him his big break. Jack Crawford was an Irish immigrant who had worked in the coal mines of Pennsylvania. After moving west following the Civil War, he apparently found employment as a janitor at the *Omaha Daily Bee*. By the time of the gold rush to Lakota lands that precipitated Custer's last campaign, he had become the paper's Black Hills correspondent. When Lakota resistance began, he set himself up as chief of a hastily organized volunteer company of scouts, but he did little (if any) scouting. Crawford was on his way back to Omaha, seeking to persuade eastern capitalists to invest in the Black Hills, when the Lakotas defeated Custer.[50] At the end of July, outfitted in buckskin by his employers at the *Bee,* he went west to join the Fifth Cavalry and Buffalo Bill. When Buffalo Bill departed in mid-campaign to resume his stage career, he recommended Captain Jack to succeed him as chief of scouts. In September Crawford was fired for leaving the command to deliver dispatches to the *New York Herald*. But the *Herald* advanced Captain Jack's celebrity by publishing his own story of the ride. That winter Captain Jack joined Buffalo Bill on the stage.[51]

Buffalo Bill and Captain Jack created malleable combinations of experience and staged fiction. The 1877 program recounted how Buffalo Bill had sent Captain Jack a dispatch informing him of Custer's death, which in turn had supposedly occasioned Captain Jack's rather confused poem,

BUFFALO BILL AND CAPTAIN JACK.

The following dispatch which was sent from Buffalo Bill to Captain Jack, and prompted the following verses from the Poet Scout, (as he is familiarly known on the frontier,) explains itself.

CAMP ON INDIAN CREEK, JULY 8TH, 1876.

"Jack, old boy, have you heard of the death of brave Custer."—BUFFALO BILL.

CUSTER'S DEATH.

Did I hear the news from Custer ?
  Well, I reckon I did, old pard ;
It came like a streak of lightnin',
  And, you bet, it hit me hard.
I ain't no hand to blubber,
  And the briny ain't run for years ;
But chalk me down for a lubber,
  If I didn't shed regular tears.

What for ? Now look you here, Bill,
  You're a bully boy, that's true;
As good as e'er wore buckskin,
  Or fought with the boys in blue ;
But I'll bet my bottom dollar
  Ye had no trouble to muster
A tear, or perhaps a hundred,
  When ye heard of the death of Custer.

He always thought well of you, pard,
  And had it been heaven's will,
In a few more days you'd met him,
  And he'd welcome his old scout Bill.
For if ye remember at Hat Creek,
  I met ye with General Carr ;
We talked of the brave young Custer,
  And recounted his deeds of war.

But little we knew even then, pard,
  (And that's just two weeks ago),
How little we dreamed of disaster,
  Or that he had met the foe—
That the fearless, reckless hero,
  So loved by the whole frontier,
Had died on the field of battle
  In this, our centennial year.

I served with him in the army,
  In the darkest days of the war :
And I recken ye know his record,
  For he was our guiding star ;
And the boys who gathered round him
  To charge in the early morn,
War just like the brave who perished
  With him on the Little Horn.

And where is the satisfaction,
  And how are we going to get square ?
By giving the reds more rifles ?
  Invite them to take more hair ?

We want no scouts, no trappers,
  Nor men who know the frontier ;
Phil, old boy, you're mistaken,
  We must have the volunteer.

Never mind that two hundred thousand,
  But give us a hundred instead ;
Send five thousand men towards Reno,
  And soon we won't leave a red.
It will save Uncle Sam lots of money,
  In fortress we need not invest,
Jest wollup the devils this summer,
  And the miners will do all the rest.

The Black Hills are now filled with miners,
  The Big Horn will soon be as full,
And which will present the most danger
  To Crazy Horse and Old Sitting Bull ?
A band of ten thousand frontier men,
  Or a couple of forts with a few
Of the boys in the East now enlisting—
  Friend Cody, I leave it with you.

They talk about peace with these demons
  By feeding and clothing them well :
I'd as soon think an angel from heaven
  Would reign with contentment in h—l.
And some day these Quakers will answer
  Before the great Judge of us all,
For the death of the daring young Custer
  And the boys who around him did fall.

Perhaps I am judging them harshly,
  But I mean what I'm telling ye, pard ;
I'm letting them down mighty easy,
  Perhaps they may think it is hard.
But I tell you the day is approaching—
  The boys are beginning to muster—
That day of the great retribution,
  The day of revenge for our Custer.

And I will be with you, friend Cody,
  My weight will go in with the boys ;
I shared all their hardships last winter,
  I shared all their sorrows and joys ;
So tell them I'm coming, friend William,
  I trust I will meet you ere long;
Regards to the boys in the mountains,
  Yours, truly, in friendship still strong.
              JACK CRAWFORD.

FRANCIS & VALENTINE,

Commercial Printing House,

No. 517 CLAY STREET,

512 to 516 Commercial Street,   San Francisco, Cal.

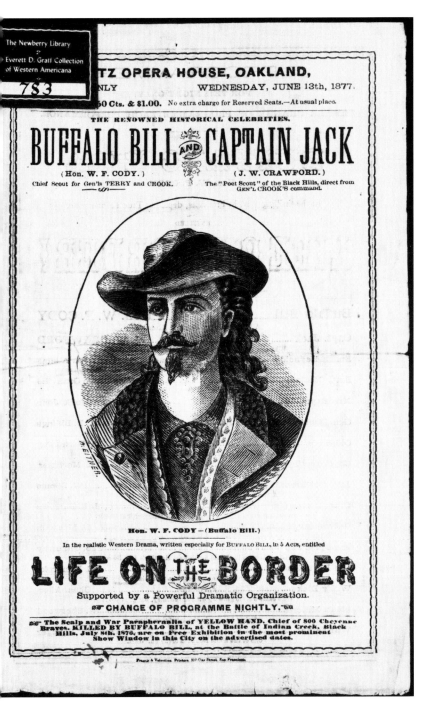

...TZ OPERA HOUSE, OAKLAND,

...NLY   WEDNESDAY, JUNE 13th, 1877.

...50 Cts. & $1.00.   No extra charge for Reserved Seats.—At usual place.

THE RENOWNED HISTORICAL CELEBRITIES,

BUFFALO BILL *and* CAPTAIN JACK

(Hon. W. F. CODY.)   (J. W. CRAWFORD.)

Chief Scout for Gen'ls TERRY and CROOK.   The "Poet Scout" of the Black Hills, direct from GEN'L CROOK'S command.

Hon. W. F. CODY — (Buffalo Bill.)

In the realistic Western Drama, written especially for BUFFALO BILL, in 5 Acts, entitled

LIFE ON THE BORDER

Supported by a Powerful Dramatic Organization.

☞ CHANGE OF PROGRAMME NIGHTLY. ☜

☞ The Scalp and War Paraphernalia of YELLOW HAND, Chief of 800 Cheyenne Braves. KILLED BY BUFFALO BILL, at the Battle of Indian Creek, Black Hills, July 8th, 1876, are on Free Exhibition in the most prominent Show Window in this City on the advertised dates.

Francis & Valentine, Printers 517 Clay Street, San Francisco.

FIGURE 16. Back and front cover of the program for Buffalo Bill and Captain Jack in *Life on the Border;* with "Custer's Death," a poem by Captain Jack Crawford (Oakland, Calif., 1877).

THE

POET SCOUT.

A BOOK OF SONG AND STORY.

BY

CAPTAIN JACK CRAWFORD,
(*Late Chief of Scouts, U. S. Army.*)

FUNK & WAGNALLS:
NEW YORK: 1886.   LONDON:
10-12 DEY STREET.   44 FLEET STREET.

FIGURE 17.   *The Poet Scout,* by Captain Jack Crawford (New York, 1886).

FIGURE 18.   Profile of George Armstrong Custer from his book *Wild Life on the Plains* (St. Louis, Mo., 1891).

"Custer's Death," published in the *Black Hills Pioneer,* August 5, 1876, and reproduced the following year in the program for Buffalo Bill's *Life on the Border* (see Figure 16). The poem demanded vengeance on "these demons" who had killed Custer. Custer's death was to be avenged by volunteers whose identity (much like Captain Jack's own) shifted according to the need of the poet. Their efforts would not "leave a red."[52] Unfortunately for Captain Jack, it was he who was playing the "red," Yellow Hand, onstage in Virginia City, reenacting the famous duel, when a drunken Buffalo Bill accidentally slashed him twice in the scripted knife fight. When he recovered, Captain Jack left the show.[53]

In poetry and onstage the basic message was clear: The slaughter of the heroic Custer justified retaliatory massacre. This inversion of aggressor and victim that justified conquest was played out over and over again. Buffalo Bill's 1893 program reprinted from *Beadle's Weekly* a poem, "Cody's Corral," by Buckskin Sam, whose last few lines read:

. . . the victors quick dismounted, and looking all around,
On their dead and mangled enemies, whose corses [*sic*] strewed the ground,
"I had sworn I would avenge them"—were the words of Buffalo Bill—
"The mothers and their infants they slew at Medicine Hill.
Our work is done—done nobly—I looked for that from you;
Boys when a cause is just, you need but stand firm and true!"[54]

Buffalo Bill and Captain Jack, linked with Custer at least tangentially through actual experience and directly through their reenactments and commemorations of his death, carried the connection one step further. They looked like Custer (Figure 18). But then Custer himself had affected the long hair and buckskin clothing of a scout; in effect, he had imitated an icon on his way to becoming one. Pictures of Buffalo Bill in profile and portraits of Custer in profile are startlingly similar, and Captain Jack, like so many western performers, mirrored both of them. The effect is not accidental. Buffalo Bill imitates Custer's pose, wears his hat, and in one representation is "surrounded" by pictures of Indians, including Sitting Bull, who fought whites.[55]

But as it turns out, the Indians who came to inhabit Buffalo Bill's version of the Custer fight had their own story to tell. At least eight Northern Cheyenne artists, for example, drew pictures of the Custer campaign in a ledger book now in the Newberry Library. These drawings depict battles and skirmishes that took place as part of the Sioux campaign of 1876, but they focus on events not featured in American accounts. In the midst of their own terrible defeat—the Mackenzie Fight at the Powder River—Northern Cheyenne artists depicted the power contained in the war bonnet and bow-lance carried by the leading man of Kit Fox Society, a Cheyenne warrior society (Figure 19). Bullets rain around him and his companions, all of whom remain unscathed.[56]

Unlike the Cheyenne artists, Amos Bad Heart Buffalo, a Lakota artist, produced, in the early twentieth century, pictures of the Custer fight itself. Basing his paintings on the accounts of warriors who had fought in the Battle of the Little Bighorn, he created a series of striking depictions. Indians on blue and green horses sweep in among the soldiers (see Plate 6). There is neither a last stand nor an exclusive focus on Custer. Instead, the battle emerges as a bloody running fight, with Lakotas, Cheyennes, and American soldiers mixed together.

Such Lakota and Cheyenne images initially existed separate from the American iconography of Custer and the Sioux campaign of 1876. Indian and white artists shared a common subject, but they understood and organized it in dramatically different ways. Within a few years of the Amos Bad Heart Buffalo paintings, some Lakota depictions of the battle began to change in a manner that suggests a convergence of American and Lakota concerns. About 1913–14 Aaron McGaffey Beede, an Episcopalian former missionary to the Sioux and a Fort Yates attorney and newspaper publisher, obtained a series of "portraits" of Custer from Indians at Standing Rock. Red Fish, a Santee-Yanktonai on the Standing Rock Reservation, drew (apparently at Beede's request) several pictures of Custer (see Plate 7).[57] Another artist, No-Two-Horn, drew a picture of Sitting Bull

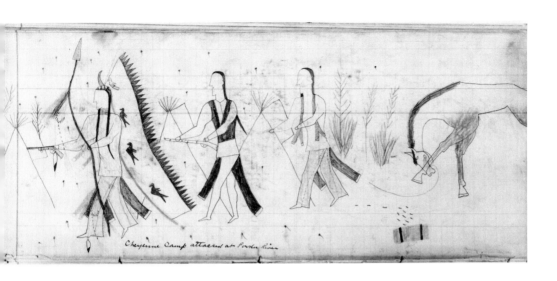

FIGURE 19. "Cheyenne Camp at-
tacked at Powder River," drawing in the
Newberry Library's "Cheyenne Ledger
Book" (no date).

and Custer on the title page of a copy of Beede's verse play *Sitting
Bull—Custer* (Figure 20). He depicted Sitting Bull, who in the play visits
Custer's corpse at sunset on the day of the battle, as being startled by
Custer's *woniya,* or spirit.[58]

It is dangerous to read too much into these intriguing and ambiguous
drawings, but it does seem clear enough that through Beede, Lakota and
American depictions of the battle entered into an interesting, if tangled,
conversation.[59] Red Fish, in one of his paintings, portrays what the historian Phil Deloria has called cultural cross-dressing. Custer, dressed as an
Indian, had, a notation on one of the pictures claims, the "tun" of an
Indian. *Tun* (or *tunj* or *ton*) is a difficult word to translate. Nineteenth-
century dictionaries render it "spirit," but for modern Lakotas it means
"of a place or of the homeland of a people." Beede argued that the Lakotas respected Custer and thought he had the spiritual power of an Indian.[60]
If this unusual claim is true, then Red Fish's depiction of him as an Indian
has a certain logic. Custer and his image were being assimilated by at least

some of the Indians at Standing Rock. Their portrayals of him as an alien in Lakota dress were similar to Amos Bad Heart Buffalo's portrayal of himself as a cowboy in white man's clothing.[61] He was an Indian cowboy; Custer was a white warrior.

Although such interpretations of the meaning Lakota artists intended can be only tentative, the association of these artists with Beede is clear and revealing.[62] Beede, claiming that his play, *Sitting Bull–Custer,* represented an Indian understanding of the conflict with Custer, incorporated into it elements of a Lakota cosmology. Custer's *woniya,* for example, predicts Sitting Bull's own death fifteen years later.[63] In response to this text, No-Two-Horn, a Lakota, drew Beede's version of a supposedly Lakota story. But No-Two-Horn's style is distinct from that of other Lakota art of

FIGURE 20.   Hand-colored photograph of painting by No-Two-Horn opposite the title page in Aaron McGaffey Beede, *Sitting Bull–Custer.* Annotated (by Beede?) as follows: "This shows S. Bull by Custer's dead body about sunset. Custer's ghost (Woniya) is departing. The Woniya of a man or a beast first assumes the form of a young tree or plant, then in time. . . ."

the time,[64] and the portrait of Custer itself appears to have been drawn from pictures available in the popular press.

We are confronted with a complicated cultural product: a Lakota drawing (by No-Two-Horn) produced in a style that borrows elements from popular illustrations to depict a scene in a white man's play written to communicate the Indians' point of view. Custer had come to be part of Sioux culture just as Sitting Bull had become part of American culture. According to Beede, the Lakotas in the early twentieth century still reported appearances of Custer's ghost along the Grand River.[65] In a complex process of cross-fertilization in the early twentieth century, Lakota stories and American stories were merging.

The signs of this cross-fertilization have left their traces in library collections. Beede sent the original drawings by Red Fish to Edward Ayer, whose collection was already part of the Newberry Library in Chicago. Someone, either Beede or Dr. N. W. Jipson, who received a shipment of Lakota art from Beede, appears to have made a photograph of the No-Two-Horn drawing and to have had it hand colored (this version is reproduced as Figure 20). It, too, found its way into the Ayer collection.[66] Whites were constantly soliciting other Indians' accounts of the battle, and the Crow scout Curley and Lakota warriors, including Rain-in-the-Face, the Lakota reputed to have killed Custer (Figure 21), provided them.[67] Ayer acquired the ledger books and paintings commemorating the battle and added them to the portraits his nephew Elbridge Ayer Burbank had painted of Lakotas and other western Indians.[68] Indian and white paintings and stories met in public and private collections in confrontations more complex, if less bloody, than those on the battlefield.

There is a nice symbolism in this meeting. In the Ayer collection Burbank's portrait of Rain-in-the-Face portrayed him in white man's dress, which in fact he often wore. In the collection, too, was Red Fish's picture of Custer in Lakota dress.[69] In different ways white representations and Lakota representations of the battle mimicked, fed on, and challenged each other. By the time of Big Bill Thompson's administration (he was mayor of Chicago from 1915 to 1923 and 1927 to 1931), a visiting Lakota

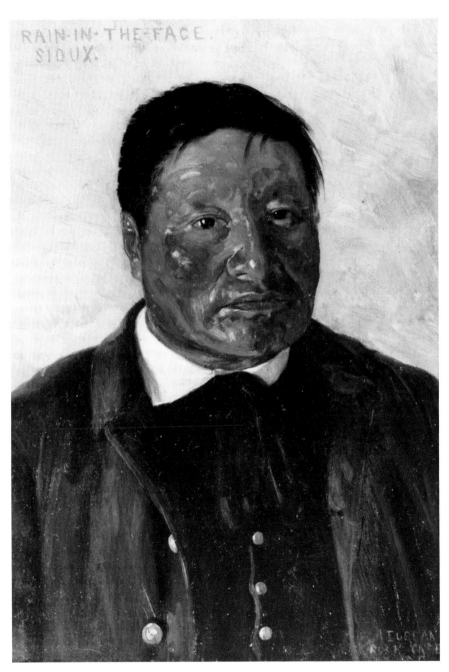

FIGURE 21. Elbridge Ayer Burbank, *Rain-in-the-Face. Sioux*. Oil on board, 1898.

delegation had him posing in a headdress as part of their campaign to change the portrayal of the Battle of the Little Bighorn in Chicago schoolbooks from an Indian massacre of whites to an American attack on Indians.[70]

The Frontier and American Identity

When the Lakotas moved to change the stories told about the Custer fight, they encountered the legacy of their old colleague Buffalo Bill.[71] For by the early twentieth century there was no way to tell stories about the West, no way to talk about an American identity, without confronting either Buffalo Bill or Turner. They had divided the narrative space of the West between them.

The division was not simple. Turner's "Significance of the Frontier" and Buffalo Bill's Wild West stand in complex and revealing relation to each other, a point we miss by trivializing Buffalo Bill and thus obscuring the common grounding of his and Turner's stories. To see Turner as serious and significant and Buffalo Bill as a charlatan and a curiosity, to see Turner as history and Buffalo Bill as entertainment, to see one as concerned with reality and the other with myth is to miss their common reliance on, and promotion of, the iconography of their time. Turner and Cody followed separate but connected strands of a single mythic cloth. And as in Chicago one hundred years ago, their seemingly contradictory stories make historical sense only when told together.

Even as they told their stories, however, Turner and Buffalo Bill shared a conviction that the experience that had produced them was no longer available: the Wild West, the frontier, was dead. And the icons of that frontier themselves became tinged with an aura of loss.

Cowboys had been part of Buffalo Bill's Wild West from its beginnings in 1882 (see Plate 8).[72] Indeed, Buffalo Bill and other Wild West showmen created the cowboy as an icon as much as they capitalized on an existing iconography. Gradually cowboys elbowed aside Indians and scouts as the main attraction in Buffalo Bill's Wild West. But they clearly dominated both the posters and the shows only in the twentieth century, when they became the representative roughriders.[73]

Many, however, felt that the actual cowboy was vanishing even as the iconographic cowboy populated the American imagination. Ironically, the cowboy became an American symbol in the very era that announced the end of the West and the closing of the frontier that had created him. Cowboys too joined the chorus: by the early twentieth century, Charlie Russell, the most thoughtful of the cowboy artists, could declare that the West was dead.[74]

For him as much as for Turner and Buffalo Bill the story of the West ended with progress killing its parents. Born of the frontier—a constant return to the primitive and natural—progress became its mortal enemy, for it eliminated the wellspring of primitivism upon which the western experience depended. The image of the future—a not altogether happy future—became the city. Russell wrote to a friend in 1916, "If I had a winter home in Hell and a summer home in Chicago I think I'd spend my summers at my winter home." There might be as many people in hell, Russell thought, but there couldn't be more smoke. Great Falls, Montana, he conceded, would one day be like Chicago, but he was glad he would not be around to see it.[75] Progress had ceased to seem desirable.

Frederick Jackson Turner, for his part, struggled to escape the pessimism that followed from his own logic. He sought equivalents to the frontier that would act as engines to create democracy and individualism. But mostly he dwelt on the challenges of a postfrontier America. On September 25, 1901, in one of a series of articles written for the *Chicago Record-Herald,* Turner analyzed the difference between earlier immigration and that of his own time:

> The immigrant of the preceding period was assimilated with comparative ease, and it can hardly be doubted that valuable contributions to American character have come from this infusion of non-English stock into the American people. But the free lands that made the process of absorption easy have gone. The immigration is

becoming increasingly more difficult of assimilation. Its competition with American labor under existing conditions may give increased power to the producer, but the effects upon American social well-being are dangerous in the extreme.

But as in so many other things, Turner's audience had in a sense anticipated his conclusions. The county histories celebrated men like Ernst Dressel: "Although not a native of America, he is loyal to the country of his adoption, and unswervingly devoted to the interest of Lenzburg Township where he has resided for many years."[76] Dressel had become an American, first, by consenting to do so and offering his loyalty and, second, by undergoing the profoundly Americanizing experience of settling new land. But with the frontier, in Turner's terms, closed, many Americans began to think that only descent from "real" Americans could now produce Americans. Genealogy, which would become an obsession of native-born Americans, was tied to this growing conviction. "Old settlers" validated not only their own but also their children's standing by identifying their families with frontier stories and frontier virtues. Indeed, Turner's own father, Andrew Jackson Turner, portrayed Columbia County, Wisconsin (Frederick Jackson Turner's boyhood home), in genealogical terms in both the title and the frontispiece (Figure 22) of *The Family Tree of Columbia County, Wis.*, the county history.

Buffalo Bill had said that the children of the pioneers inherited "the homes their fathers located and fenced for them."[77] But they inherited more than that. They inherited an American identity. What their parents had secured through experience, they secured as an inheritance; descent from true Americans had replaced the pioneers' consenting to undergo the quintessential American frontier experience. New immigrants, to whom this frontier experience was foreclosed, seemed like dangerous, exotic, and unassimilable aliens to many native-born Americans.

In lamenting the lost frontier, the primitive, and direct combat with nature, Turner, Buffalo Bill, and Russell worried not only about assimilation

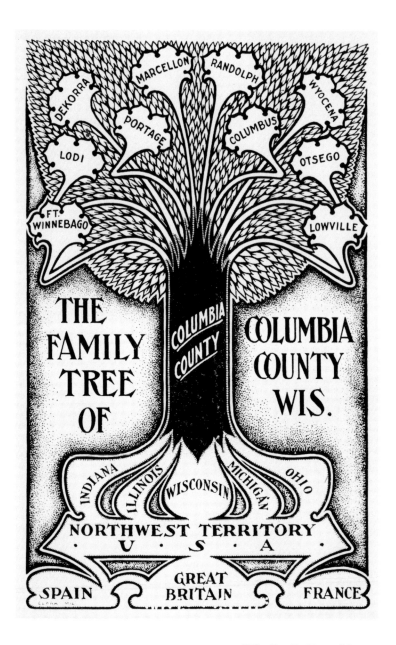

FIGURE 22. "The Family Tree of Columbia County, Wis[consin]," from the
1904 book of the same name by Andrew
Jackson Turner. Photograph courtesy of
the State Historical Society of Wisconsin.

but about manhood as well. Like most of their peers, they understood American space and American experience in gendered terms. The frontier was masculine; machines and cities were its antithesis. They emasculated men, robbed them of their true manhood. Thus cities and machines were defined as feminine. Russell confronted this issue directly:

Invention has made it easy for man kind but it has made him no

better. Machinery has no branes. A lady with manicured fingers can

drive an automobile with out maring her polished nails. But

to sit behind six range bred horses with both hands full of ribbons

these are God made animals and have branes. To drive these over a

mountain road takes both hands feet and head its no lady's job.[78]

Russell made the same point even more pithily in a painting, *The Old Story:* a car spooks a team of horses pulling a buckboard, throwing the cowboy holding the reins while the well-dressed goggled motorist in his machine looks on.[79]

In defining the frontier as both the engine of progress and the domain of real men who dominated other men and nature, Russell, Turner, and Buffalo Bill had seemingly painted themselves into a corner. The frontier story of progress had hidden within it a message of eventual decline. Progress had turned on them and trapped them. Narratives that had summarized firsts now memorialized lasts —the last "real" cowboy, the last "real" Indian, the "last" herd of buffalo—even if, as with Buffalo Bill's last show, the encores seemed to go on for years. And the encores, in a real sense, were the point. For Turner, Buffalo Bill, and Russell had both overestimated their grasp of the "real West" and underestimated the power of the stories they had created. So powerful were these that the West had become as much an American story as an American experience. The story could take on a life of its own, and a variety of other Americans attempted to place their own stories within it.

Charlie Russell had at least an inkling that this might happen. In 1917 he inscribed a drawing and a verse to a neighbor's child.

> The west is dead my Friend
> But writers hold the seed
> And what they saw
> will live and grow
> Again to those who read.[80]

But what Russell credited to writers—the ability to make the story "live and grow"—really belonged to a much wider group of Americans.

The people of the West and their actual western experiences were, of course, always much more varied and complex than those Turner or Buffalo Bill or Russell had portrayed. Only a few signs of this complexity had not vanished beneath the dominant iconography. The frontispiece of A. T. Andreas's *History of Chicago,* for example, contained the usual log cabin imagery (Figure 23). But the log cabin was that of a black man, Jean Baptiste Pointe du Sable, not a white man. And it was set not in the midst of an empty forest, but near an Indian village.[81]

The stories, like the reality, however, could contain a more diverse cast. What Buffalo Bill and Captain Jack had known, what the Indian showmen had known, was that to be a westerner or a scout or a warrior was at a certain level to inhabit a role. And assume it, occupy it, and reshape it, Americans did. Imaginative possession was not available only to showmen. Upper-class easterners, from Owen Wister (the author of *The Virginian* [1902]) to Frederic Remington to Teddy Roosevelt, created or adopted cowboy identities.[82] Roosevelt turned his quest for manhood into a western story. He was the eastern dude who became the cowboy president. He boosted his own cowboy credentials with a series of articles later published as *Ranch Life and the Hunting Trail* (1888), with illustrations by Frederic Remington in later editions.[83] As an army officer he recruited cowboys whose regimental nickname—the Rough Riders—echoed the name

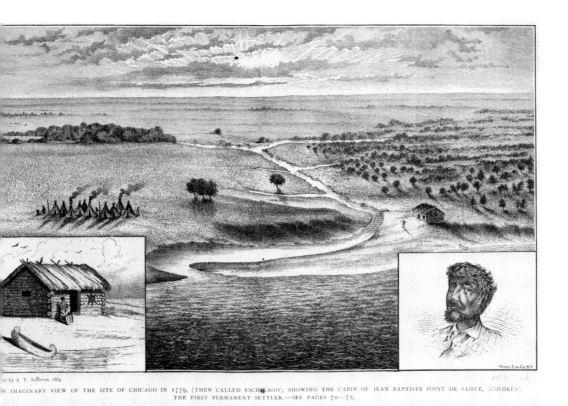

Int by A. T. Andreas. 1884

N IMAGINARY VIEW OF THE SITE OF CHICAGO IN 1779, (THEN CALLED ESCHIKAGO), SHOWING THE CABIN OF JEAN BAPTISTE POINT DE SAIBLE, (COLORED)
THE FIRST PERMANENT SETTLER.—SEE PAGES 70—72.

FIGURE 23. Frontispiece from A. T. Andreas, *History of Chicago from the Earliest Period to the Present Time* (Chicago, 1884), vol. 1.

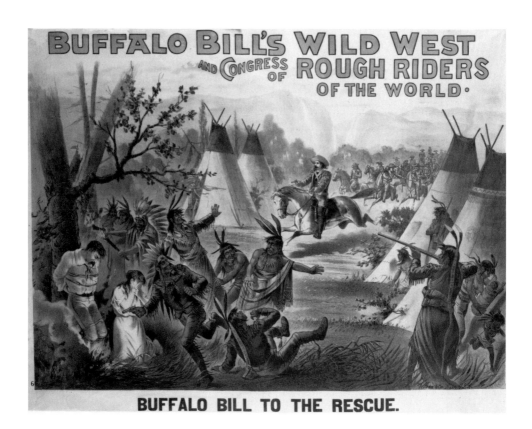

BUFFALO BILL TO THE RESCUE.

of Buffalo Bill's Wild West and Congress of Rough Riders (Figures 24, 25). His cowboy soldiers secured as a gift for Roosevelt a bronze sculpture by Remington—*The Bronco Buster*—that Roosevelt had long admired. Indeed, the cowboy on the bronco looked like Roosevelt, or perhaps vice versa.[84]

The West of Remington, Roosevelt, and Wister was an unabashedly masculine and nasty place, the domain of Anglo-Saxon men bent on keeping all they regarded as lesser breeds in their place. Wister, Remington, and Roosevelt sought to populate their stories of the West largely with men like themselves. But the stories also slipped from their grasp, just as they had escaped the control of Turner and Buffalo Bill. The stories became contested. They could be inhabited by the very people Remington, Roosevelt, and Wister despised or marginalized: non-whites, immigrants, and women. This initial repopulation of the Wild West was largely imaginative.

FIGURE 24 (*opposite*). *To the Rescue.* Poster advertising Buffalo Bill's Wild West (Baltimore, 1894). Photograph courtesy of the Buffalo Bill Museum, Cody, Wyoming.

FIGURE 25 (*left*). Eduard Holst, *The Charge of the Rough Riders: Grand Galop Militaire*, 1898.

In various fictions, for example, women inhabited roles and representations once occupied by white native-born males. This colonization—a kind of cultural cross-dressing—had appeared with Annie Oakley in Buffalo Bill's Wild West, but it was also apparent in popular fiction even as Russell lamented the death of the West. Florence Ryerson's story "The Codfish and the Cattle Princess," which appeared in the September 1918 edition of *Sunset,* was illustrated with a picture in which a woman in cowboy clothes stood before a seated man, their horses in the background. The caption read: "He didn't know any girls at home who dressed like men and could talk to a fellow in this frank and unconscious fashion." Similar images showed up in advertising—as in the famous Jordan automobile advertisement of a "broncho-busting, steer-roping girl"—and later in the movies (see Plate 9).[85]

Americans, however, did not simply view such representations. They were invited, as consumers, to reenact the stories, and they accepted the invitation. A common convention in the early road maps, for example, was that tourists followed in the path of the pioneers, encountering in some sense what the settlers and scouts had encountered (see Plate 10). Preserved frontier sites or, better yet, newly constructed ones, such as Frontierland in Disneyland or the western town at Knott's Berry Farm, opened opportunities for children, and indeed adults, to reenact western stories.

Such reenactments, such inhabiting of the roles of frontier stories, became a part of most American childhoods. American children dressed as cowboys and Indians. As play space and performance space, the West was fully populated with Jewish and Catholic, African American and Latino, Polish American, Italian American, male and female cowboys and Indians. This imaginative West was a startlingly diverse place.

But so, in fact, was the nineteenth-century West. To be fair to Buffalo Bill, he had recognized this. His Wild West had Indians. It had Annie Oakley. It had Mexican vaqueros such as Vincent Orapeza and Antonio Esquivel.[86] Turner, too, of course, had recognized diversity. Although he paid far less attention to non-whites and women, his West had been full of non-English-speaking Europeans whose frontier experience had created an American identity.

In a real sense the imaginative creation of a diverse and performative West, one with more roots in Buffalo Bill than in Turner, prepared the way for a new history that reexamined actual lived nineteenth-century experience in a West much more diverse than that of the Turnerian story. Like Turner and Cody, late-twentieth-century historians have drawn on their world. They have worked from the icons, representations, symbols, images, and possible stories already present in their culture. New Western Histories challenge both the narratives of Buffalo Bill's conquest and the Turnerian story of an advance into an empty continent. They seek to portray an experience more varied and complicated than Buffalo Bill or Turner or Russell had provided.

These stories we tell about the West matter. They not only reveal how we think about ourselves but also help determine how we choose to act toward each other.

Both Turner and Buffalo Bill were storytellers, but neither was content to be a mere storyteller. Each claimed to be an educator, a historian—to represent in his story an actual past. The stories they told were not so much invented (although there was some of that) as selected from the past, with the authors erasing images that did not fit. Such selectivity was necessary, for the past itself is not a story; it is the raw material from which we make coherent stories, not all of them factual. We can, within the repertoire of stories our culture provides, tell any story we want, but not all representations of the past can stand up against the evidence we can recover of real past events and real people.

These stories told about the frontier and the West have certainly not always been told with democratic intent, but they have sometimes had democratic consequences. Attempts to close them off, to claim them for certain groups, have failed. They have become democratic stories inhabited by diverse Americans and open to multiple retellings—but at a price. For to tell so many stories of this kind is to cut off the telling of other stories, other narratives, other imaginings.

In any nation's history there can come a time for new stories, but in a country as diverse as the United States the long dominance of this central imaginative narrative of the frontier has had significant virtues. In a country with so many variants of actual experience, it is perhaps a good thing to find imaginative coherence in a set of stories that accept change and conflict as givens. When we all mount up, when we assume the right to inhabit and retell a common past, then there seems to be a unity among us that transcends, without erasing, our differences.

Notes

1. Frederick Jackson Turner, "The Significance of the Frontier in American History," *Annual Report of the American Historical Association for the Year 1893* (Washington, D.C.: Government Printing Office, 1894), 199–227. For details regarding Turner's formulation of the frontier thesis and his appearance in Chicago, see Ray Allen Billington, *Frederick Jackson Turner: Historian, Teacher, Scholar* (New York: Oxford University Press, 1973), 82–131.

2. See the advertisement in the *Chicago Tribune,* April 27, 1893.

3. The standard biography of Buffalo Bill is Don Russell, *The Lives and Legends of Buffalo Bill* (Norman: University of Oklahoma Press, 1960). Russell has also written the most comprehensive study of Wild West shows, *The Wild West; or, A History of the Wild West Shows, . . .* (Fort Worth, Tex.: Amon Carter Museum of Western Art, 1970). For a discussion of Buffalo Bill and Turner, see also Richard Slotkin, *Gunfighter Nation: The Myth of the Frontier in Twentieth-Century America* (New York: Atheneum, 1992), 67.

4. *Buffalo Bill's Wild West and Congress of Rough Riders of the World* (Chicago, 1893), 9.

5. Richard Slotkin, *Gunfighter Nation,* 55–59, 66–87. For Buffalo Bill's invitation to the historians, see Billington, *Frederick Jackson Turner,* 127.

6. *Buffalo Bill's Wild West and Congress of Rough Riders of the World,* 4.

7. Slotkin, *Gunfighter Nation,* 14, 75.

8. *Buffalo Bill's Wild West and Congress of Rough Riders of the World,* 22.

9. Turner, "Significance," 199.

10. *Buffalo Bill's Wild West and Congress of Rough Riders of the World,* 4.

11. Sarah J. Blackstone has compiled a revealing selection of Buffalo Bill's business correspondence, including his efforts in irrigation, mining, and western resorts (*The Business of Being Buffalo Bill* [New York: Praeger, 1988]; see, for example, 44–45, 55–61).

12. *Buffalo Bill's Wild West and Congress of Rough Riders of the World,* 10.

13. Ibid., 10.

14. Albert Richardson, *Beyond the Mississippi: From the Great River to the Great Ocean . . .* (Hartford, Conn.: American Publishing Company, 1867), i. Proclamations of the centrality of the frontier were a staple of mid- and late-nineteenth-century writing: see Justin Winsor, *Narrative and Critical History of America* (1888); Theodore Roosevelt, *The Winning of the West,* 4 vols. (New York: Putnam, 1889), 1:1; Henry Howe, *Historical Collections for the Great West* (Cincinnati, Ohio: Henry Howe, 1856), 7–8. Howe's book went through numerous editions and had sold eighty thousand copies by 1860. This "extraordinary sale" demonstrated the public interest in the frontier; see the preface to the enlarged edition (Howe, *The Great West* [New York: George F. Tuttle, 1860]), viii.

15. Ray Allen Billington, *Frederick Jackson Turner,* 130.

16. See my "Frederick Jackson Turner," in *Historians of the American Frontier: A Bio-Bibliographical Sourcebook,* ed. John Wunder (Greenwood, Conn.: Greenwood Press, 1988), 664–65.

17. Henry Nash Smith, *Virgin Land: The American West as Symbol and Myth* (1950; rpt. Cambridge: Harvard University Press, 1970), 251.

18. For Pawnee Bill and other Wild West shows see Russell, *The Wild West,* 32–33, 50–52, 75–76, 98–103, 129–33.

19. *Buffalo Bill's Wild West and Congress of Rough Riders of the World,* 7. For Cody's birthdate, see Russell, *Lives and Legends of Buffalo Bill,* 6.

20. Turner, "Significance," 199.

21. Turner, "Significance," 199–227. My emphasis here is on Turner's talk in Chicago in 1893. I have given a wider analysis of Turner's historical thinking in "Frederick Jackson Turner," 660–81.

22. Turner, "Significance," 201.

23. Ibid., 216.

24. Ibid., 208.

25. Bingham's painting, as Nancy Rash has emphasized, was notable for its featuring of pioneer families. Rash details its initial disappointing reception and its subsequent mass reproduction as a print (*The Painting and Politics of George Caleb Bingham* [New Haven, Conn.: Yale University Press, 1991], 60–65).

26. Turner, "Significance," 200–201.

27. See the map by J. C. Jeager, *Schauplatz des Kriegs zwischen Engelland und seinen Collonien in America . . .* , 1776, Newberry Library.

28. "Westward Ho," in *The Complete Poetical Works of Joaquin Miller* (San Francisco: Whitaker and Ray Co., 1897), 187–88.

29. Turner, "Significance," 201.

30. For *The Squatters* (1850), see Rash, *Painting and Politics,* 58–60.

31. See Edward Pessen, *The Log Cabin Myth: The Social Backgrounds of the Presidents* (New Haven, Conn.: Yale University Press, 1984), 10–26.

32. Samuel W. Durant, *History of Ingham and Eaton Counties* (Philadelphia: D. W. Ensign, 1880), facing 222. The county histories of the D. W. Ensign Company were not the only ones to employ this symbolism. See also *History of Calhoun County, Michigan* (Philadelphia: Everts, 1877), facing 185.

33. The poster was reproduced in 1974 by Historic Urban Plans, Ithaca, N.Y., from a lithograph in its collections.

34. Turner, "Significance," 200.

35. James W. Steele, *The Sons of the Border* (Topeka, Kans., 1873), 9.

36. See, for example, J. L. McConnel, *Western Characters* (New York: Redfield, 1853), 109–37.

37. *Chicago Tribune,* April 27, 1893, p. 2, and advertisement, same issue. See the illustrations and stories throughout the program *Buffalo Bill's Wild West and Congress of Rough Riders of the World.*

38. *Buffalo Bill's Wild West and Congress of Rough Riders of the World.* See also Don Russell, *The Wild West,* 27, 46.

39. Turner, "Significance," 38.

40. See, for example, Colonel Frank Triplett, *Conquering the Wilderness* (New York: N. D. Thompson, 1883), 62.

41. *Chicago Tribune,* June 14 and 16, 1893; July 27, 1893. In each case careful readers would discover that the first act of violence had been by whites.

42. For an analysis of visual representations of Custer's battle, see Brian Dippie, *Custer's Last Stand: The Anatomy of an American Myth* (Missoula: University

of Montana Press, 1976). For a fine discussion of the portrayal of the Custer fight in the movies, see Paul Hutton, "'Correct in Every Detail': General Custer in Hollywood," *Montana; The Magazine of Western History* 41, no. 1 (Winter 1991): 28–57. See also Don Russell, *Custer's Last; or, The Battle of the Little Big Horn in Picturesque Perspective . . .* (Fort Worth, Tex.: Amon Carter Museum of Western Art, 1968). For the cultivation of the Custer myth and its uses, see Richard Slotkin, *Fatal Environment: The Myth of the Frontier in the Age of Industrialization, 1800–1890* (New York: Atheneum, 1985).

43. There are several copies of this photograph in the Elmo Scott Watson Collection, box 15 (Sitting Bull, Totanka i-Yotanka, Hunk papa Sioux folder), Edward E. Ayer Collection, Newberry Library.

44. Russell, *The Wild West,* 24, 44, 47, 65.

45. For Yellow Hand, see Russell, *The Lives and Legends of Buffalo Bill,* 215, 219–35. The name supposedly should be translated Yellow Hair. There is still controversy over the translation.

46. Russell, *The Lives and Legends of Buffalo Bill,* 231.

47. Slotkin, *Gunfighter Nation,* 72.

48. For an account of *Life on the Border* in the East and the attack on the display of the scalp, see Russell, *The Lives and Legends of Buffalo Bill,* 254–55. According to Father Peter Powell, who has worked with the Northern Cheyenne for years, the style of some of the beadwork in the headdress Buffalo Bill captured from Yellow Hand/Yellow Hair dates to a time after his death. Buffalo Bill might later have repaired or altered the headdress, or he might have had it manufactured for his show.

49. For Buffalo Bill posters, see Jack Rennert, *One Hundred Posters of Buffalo Bill's Wild West* (New York: Darien House, 1976).

50. Captain Jack Crawford, letter, dated July 13, 1876, published in the *Black Hills Pioneer,* August 12, 1876, p. 1. I would like to thank Brian Dippie for sending me copies of Crawford's letters to the *Black Hills Pioneer.*

51. See Darlis A. Miller's biography, *Captain Jack Crawford: Buckskin Poet, Scout, and Showman* (Albuquerque: University of New Mexico Press, 1993), 1–65. Her account is at variance with the memories of Crawford's employer, but

his letter about Captain Jack was written long after the events it recounts. See the letter from Alfred Sorenson to Elmo Scott Watson, dated May 23, 1938, in the Elmo Scott Watson Collection, box 10 (Crawford, Captain Jack folder), Edward E. Ayer Collection, Newberry Library.

52. Darlis Miller (*Captain Jack Crawford,* 52–53) believes that Captain Jack actually did receive a dispatch from Buffalo Bill that prompted him to write the poem, but this is doubtful. There is no evidence that Captain Jack knew Buffalo Bill before joining the Fifth Cavalry. It is hard to understand how Buffalo Bill would have known Captain Jack was in Omaha or why he would have sent him a telegram about an event that was national news. It seems far more likely that Captain Jack read of Custer's defeat and wrote the poem. Captain Jack was peeved because General Phil Sheridan had refused the services of volunteers in avenging Custer's death (letter from Captain Jack to the editor of the *Black Hills Pioneer,* dated July 13, 1876, and published August 12, p. 1).

53. Miller, *Captain Jack Crawford,* 74–75. The next night Buffalo Bill played both himself and Captain Jack.

54. Buckskin Sam, "Cody's Corral; or, The Scouts and the Sioux," *Buffalo Bill's Wild West and Congress of Rough Riders of the World,* 12.

55. See, for example, the pictures of Buffalo Bill in Rennert, *One Hundred Posters of Buffalo Bill's Wild West,* 33, 71, and compare them to the picture of Custer reproduced in Glenn Bradley, *Winning of the Southwest* (Chicago: H. C. McClurg, 1912), facing 174, and my Figure 20. For Custer in buckskin in a hunter's pose, see Elmo Scott Watson Collection, box 6 (Custer Pictures folder), Edward E. Ayer Collection, Newberry Library. For a similar picture of Buffalo Bill, see *The West of Buffalo Bill: Frontier Art, Indian Crafts, Memorabilia from the Buffalo Bill Historical Center* (New York: Abrams, [1974]), 15. For Captain Jack's cultivation of the image, see Figure 17 and the photograph entitled "Capt. Jack Crawford, Poet-Scout of the Black Hills," Watson Collection, Ayer Collection, Newberry Library.

56. Indians initially worried about the consequences of their representations if they came into white hands. Before they sold the ledger book now in the

Edward E. Ayer Collection of the Newberry Library, unknown Cheyennes redrew some of the figures of the soldiers, ineffectively disguising them as Crow Indians so as not to offend whites with pictures of dead soldiers. I would like to thank Father Peter Powell, who has worked for years on Cheyenne ledger book art and helped me to understand the significance of the scenes and figures represented. Any mistakes made in this interpretation are my own.

57. The Red Fish who drew these pictures appears to be the same Red Fish (Hogan'-Lu'Ta) who acted as an informant for Frances Densmore; see her *Teton Sioux Music,* Bureau of American Ethnology, Bulletin 61 (Washington, D.C.: Government Printing Office, 1918), 91. Fort Yates was the headquarters of the Standing Rock Agency. For an account of the drawings and their subsequent sale, see the letter from Aaron McGaffey Beede to Dr. N. W. Jipson, January 4, 1922, in Sioux Indian Drawings, Fort Yates, Edward E. Ayer Art Collection. Beede explains how he commissioned the art during what he called the terrible "starving time" of 1913–14 among the Lakotas at Standing Rock.

58. The location of the original edition painted by No-Two-Horn is unknown. A photographically reproduced edition of Aaron McGaffey Beede's *Sitting Bull–Custer* (Bismarck, N.D.: Bismarck Tribune Company, 1913), is in the Edward E. Ayer Collection, Newberry Library. Beede gives an account of the origin of the drawing in "'The Custer Massacre,' an Address by Judge Aaron McGaffey Beede of Fort Yates, North Dakota, before the Chicago Historical Society, November 23, 1922," typescript, Ayer Collection, Newberry Library, 15–17.

59. Without the accompanying notations and the descriptions, Red Fish's pictures would appear to be portraits of Lakotas and of a mounted white man. There is nothing in the figures themselves to suggest that they are Custer. But all the figures are labeled Custer. In one Custer seems dressed as much like a cowboy as a cavalry man, but the caption says that he has the "tonj" of an Indian. *Ton* (or *tun* or *tunj*) translates as "the power to do supernatural things"; it is the spiritual essence of a person. See James R. Walker, *Lakota Belief and Ritual,* ed. Raymond J. DeMallie and Elaine A. Jahner (Lincoln:

University of Nebraska Press, 1980), 95, 127. I would like to thank Ray DeMallie for explaining Lakota concepts to me.

60. See Beede, *Sitting Bull–Custer,* title page and 31–33, and Beede, "The Custer Massacre," 9, for Lakota respect for Custer.

61. Amos Bad Heart Buffalo, in fact, sometimes worked as a cowboy. See Leslie Tillet, ed., *Wind on the Buffalo Grass: The Indians' Own Account of the Battle at the Little Big Horn River, and the Death of Their Life on the Plains* (New York: Thomas Y. Crowell, 1976), xv; Hartley Burr Alexander, ed., *Sioux Indian Paintings, Part II: The Art of Amos Bad Heart Buffalo* (Nice: C. Szwedzicki, 1938), 5.

62. Among other possible interpretations are that Red Fish might simply have labeled existing figures as Custer to please Beede and that his paintings might be an elaborate joke, a deception of white people. Or Beede may have mistranslated: Red Fish may, for example, have been offering a drawing of Custer's Arikara scouts rather than one of Custer himself.

63. Walker, *Lakota Belief and Ritual,* 70–71. *Woniya* refers to a spirit when it dwells in a human being. A *wanagi* or *woniya* is a spirit that has once been a human spirit.

64. Sioux Indian Drawings, Fort Yates Collection, Edward E. Ayer Collection, Newberry Library.

65. For the merging of Lakota and American stories, see Beede, *Sitting Bull–Custer* (Newberry Library copy), 31–33; for reports of sitings of Custer's ghost, see Beede, "The Custer Massacre," 9.

66. Letter from Beede to Jipson, January 4, 1922, Edward E. Ayer Art Collection, Newberry Library. The picture itself was donated by Jipson.

67. Rain-in-the-Face (who was also at the Columbian Exposition; he did not claim to have killed Custer) and Curley, among others, were the objects of considerable press attention (Beede, "The Custer Massacre," 31). Elbridge Ayer Burbank portraits of participants in the battle, now in the Ayer Collection, illustrated several of these accounts. See, for example, Charles A. Eastman (Ohiyesa), "Rain-in-the-Face: The Story of a Sioux Warrior," *Outlook,* October 27, 1906, 507–12. Ohiyesa was Eastman's original Santee name.

See also clipping file, Indians–Chiefs–Rain-in-the-Face, Elmo Scott Watson Collection, box 15, Edward E. Ayer Collection, Newberry Library. For Curley and his stories and accounts in the popular press, see the folder labeled Indian Wars–Custer Scouts–Crow–Curley, Watson Collection, box 6, Edward E. Ayer Collection, Newberry Library. See also Hamlin Garland, "General Custer's Last Fight As Seen by Two Moon: The Battle Described by a Chief Who Took Part in It," *McClure's Magazine* 11, no. 5 (September 1898): 443–48. The 1891 reissue of Custer's *Life on the Plains* also contained reproductions of a ledger book with drawings by Sitting Bull (*Wild Life on the Plains,* 381–85). For a modern collection of Indian accounts and art of the Little Bighorn, see Tillet, ed., *Wind on the Buffalo Grass.*

68. Charles Francis Browne, "Elbridge Ayer Burbank: A Painter of Indian Portraits," *Brush and Pencil: An Illustrated Magazine of the Arts and Crafts* 3 (1898): 17–35.

69. A photograph of Burbank's painting was used as an illustration in Hamlin Garland's article "General Custer's Last Fight," *McClure's Magazine* (as in note 67).

70. "Custer's Last Battle in New Light," undated clipping, Elmo Scott Watson Collection, Edward E. Ayer Collection, Newberry Library.

71. Many Lakotas appear to have been quite fond of Buffalo Bill and to have enjoyed their life as showmen. Jack Red Cloud forwarded a resolution of the Oglala council to Mrs. Cody to express their sympathy on news of his death. They had, the letter said, "found in Buffalo Bill a warm and lasting friend" (Blackstone, *The Business of Being Buffalo Bill,* 84).

72. Russell, *The Wild West,* 2–3.

73. For another representation of the cowboy in the 1880s, see Bob Grantham Quickfall, *Western Life and How I Became a Bronco Buster* (London: J. W. Wright, c. 1890), cover. Remington added representations of cowboys to his portraits of western life. See, for example, his illustration in *Harper's Weekly* 33 (1889): 1016–17. See also the work of the cowboy artists Charlie Russell and Will James; James's illustrated books include *All in the Day's Riding* (New York: Scribner, 1936) and *The Drifting Cowboy* (New York: Scribner, 1925).

74. "The West Is Dead My Friend," in Elizabeth A. Dear, ed., *Regards to the Bunch: Letters, Poems, and Illustrations of C. M. Russell* (Great Falls, Mont.: C. M. Russell Museum, 1992), p. 40. See also Brian Dippie, ed., *"Paper Talk": Charlie Russell's American West* (New York: Knopf, 1979), 124–25.

75. Russell to "Friend Trigg," February 24, 1916, in Dear, ed., *Regards to the Bunch,* 26; Dippie, ed., *"Paper Talk,"* 122–23.

76. *Portrait and Biographical Record of St. Clair County, Illinois* (Chicago: Chapman Bros., 1892), 525.

77. *Buffalo Bill's Wild West and Congress of Rough Riders of the World,* 10.

78. Russell to "Friend Bob [Thoroughman]," April 14, 1920, in Dear, ed., *Regards to the Bunch,* 31.

79. *The Old Story,* watercolor, 15¾″ × 20″, signed and dated lower left, 1910, C. M. Russell Museum, Great Falls, Montana. There is a print in Ray W. Steele and Pam Yascavage, eds., *The C. M. Russell Museum Permanent Collection Catalog* (Great Falls, Mont.: C. M. Russell Museum, 1989), 13.

80. "The West Is Dead My Friend," in Dear, ed., *Regards to the Bunch,* 40.

81. Other iconographic representations of the founding of Chicago featured John Kinzie, a white man, rather than du Sable.

82. See G. Edward White, *The Eastern Establishment and the Western Experience: The West of Frederic Remington, Theodore Roosevelt, and Owen Wister* (New Haven, Conn.: Yale University Press, 1968). Remington, along with Charles Russell, illustrated an edition of *The Virginian* (New York: Macmillan, 1911). He also illustrated two editions of Theodore Roosevelt's *Ranch Life and the Hunting Trail* (London: Unwin, 1896; New York: Century Co., 1901).

83. Roosevelt claimed a frontier identity in the preface to his four-volume *Winning of the West,* 1:xiv (as in note 14).

84. Douglas Allen, *Frederic Remington and the Spanish-American War* (New York: Crown, 1971), 133–35.

85. See *Vanity Fair,* July 1923, and the *Saturday Evening Post,* July 23, 1923. For a discussion of the West, gender, and automobile advertising, particularly the influential Jordan advertisements, see R. A. Corrigan, "Somewhere West of

Laramie, on the Road to West Egg: Automobiles, Fillies, and the West in *The Great Gatsby*," *Journal of Popular Culture* 7 (Summer 1973): 152–58. Relevant movies include Columbia Pictures' *Renegades* ("The Red-Blooded Story of a Red-Headed Girl . . . riding with the Dembrows . . . the West's most notorious outlaw band") and, of course, *Johnny Guitar,* with Joan Crawford.

86. Russell, *Lives and Legends of Buffalo Bill,* 377.

CALIFORNIA.
Its Past History
ITS PRESENT POSITION
ITS FUTURE PROSPECTS.

SCENE ON A BRANCH OF THE SACRAMENTO.

London,
Printed for the Booksellers.
1850.

PLATE I. Frontispiece
and title page for *California:
Its Past History, Its Present
Position, Its Future Prospects,*
attributed to G. A. Fleming
(London, 1850).

PLATE 2. Detail of a map showing
the route of the Mormon pioneers from
Nauvoo to Great Salt Lake [1899].

BUFFALO BILL'S DUEL WITH YELLOW HAND.

PLATE 3.   Buffalo Bill with Yellow
Hand's scalp, from J. W. Buel, *Heroes
of the Plains; or, Life and Wonderful
Adventures of Wild Bill, Buffalo Bill and
Exploits* . . . (St. Louis, Missouri, 1881).

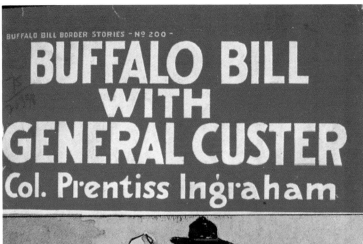

PLATE 4. Cover of a dime novel by
Colonel Prentiss Ingraham (New York,
1914).

BUFFALO BILL TO THE RESCUE.

STORY of the

WILD WEST

AND
CAMP-FIRE CHATS,

BY
BUFFALO BILL,
(HON. W. F. CODY.)

A FULL AND COMPLETE HISTORY OF THE RENOWNED PIONEER QUARTETTE,

BOONE, CROCKETT, CARSON AND BUFFALO BILL.

Replete with Graphic Descriptions of Wild Life and Thrilling Adventures by Famous Heroes of the Frontier.

A Record of Exciting Events on the Western Borders Pushed Westward
to the Sea: Massacres, Desperate Battles, Extraordinary Bravery,
Marvelous Fortitude, Astounding Heroism, Grand Hunts,
Savage Encounters, Adventures by Flood and Field,
Rollicking Anecdotes, Tales of Sorrow, Droll
Stories, Curious Escapades, and a Melange
of Incidents that make up the Melodrama of Civilization in its March
over Mountains and Prairies
to the Pacific.

INCLUDING A DESCRIPTION OF

BUFFALO BILL'S CONQUESTS IN ENGLAND

WITH HIS WILD WEST EXHIBITION, WHERE ROYALTY FROM ALL THE EUROPEAN
NATIONS PAID HIM A GENEROUS HOMAGE AND MADE HIS WONDERFUL
SHOW THE GREATEST SUCCESS OF MODERN TIMES.

SUPERBLY ILLUSTRATED WITH
250 ORIGINAL ILLUSTRATIONS
MADE ESPECIALLY FOR THE BOOK.

HISTORICAL PUBLISHING COMPANY,
Philadelphia, Pa.

PLATE 5. Frontispiece and title page of *Story of the Wild West and Camp-Fire Chats,* by Buffalo Bill (Philadelphia, 1888).

PLATE 6.   Scene from the Battle of the
Little Big Horn, by Amos Bad Heart
Buffalo, from *Sioux Indian Paintings,
Part 2: The Art of Amos Bad Heart Buffalo,*
edited by Hartley Burr Alexander (Nice,
1938).

PLATE 7. Hogan'-Lu'Ta (Red Fish),
painting of "Custer as a Comanche . . ."
(no date).

REPRESENTATION OF LIFE IN A COW CAMP.

PLATE 8 (*above*).   Frontispiece from
*A Texas Cow Boy; or, Fifteen Years on the
Hurricane Deck of a Spanish Pony,* by
Charles Siringo (Chicago, 1886).

PLATE 9 (*opposite*). This Jordan
automobile advertisement appeared in
the *Saturday Evening Post,* July 23, 1923.

Fred Cole

Somewhere West of Laramie

SOMEWHERE west of Laramie there's a broncho-busting, steer-roping girl who knows what I'm talking about. She can tell what a sassy pony, that's a cross between greased lightning and the place where it hits, can do with eleven hundred pounds of steel and action when he's going high, wide and handsome.

The truth is—the Jordan Playboy was built for her.

JORDAN

JORDAN MOTOR CAR COMPANY, Inc., Cleveland, Ohio

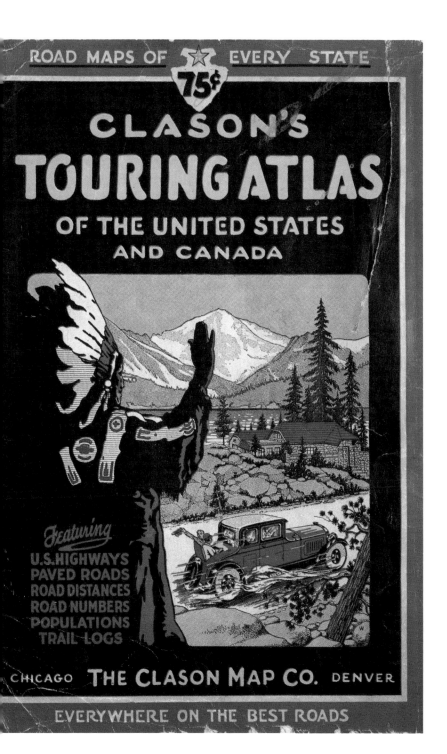

PLATE 10.   Cover of *Clason's Touring
Atlas of the United States and Canada*
(Chicago [1920]).

PATRICIA NELSON LIMERICK

THE ADVENTURES OF THE FRONTIER IN THE TWENTIETH CENTURY

Travels in Frontierland

THE YEAR 1988 SIGNIFIED THE fortieth anniversary of humanity's escape from zippers and buttons. In May of that year a journal of science and technology called *Discover* published an article commemorating this occasion. "Velcro," the headline read: "The Final Frontier."

To the specialist in Western American history, this is a title to ponder. In what sense might Velcro constitute a frontier? In his 1893 essay "The Significance of the Frontier in American History," Frederick Jackson Turner left his central term curiously befogged: The word "frontier," he said, "is an elastic one, and for our purposes does not need sharp definition."[1] But Turner did join the director of the United States census in offering one clear and concrete definition: the frontier was a place occupied by fewer than two people per square mile. Thus, if the headline writer were a strict follower of Turner's quantitative definition, then the Velcro Frontier would be a place where fewer than two people per square mile used Velcro. The writer, on the other hand, might have been following one of the more poetic and less precise Turnerian definitions, finding in a society's choice of fasteners a symbolic line of division between wilderness and human culture, backwardness and progress, savagery and civilization. The habit-bound users of zippers would now represent the primitive and backward people of North America, with the hardy, adventurous users of Velcro living on the cutting edge of progress.

Historians of the American West might puzzle over the shifting definitions of the word "frontier," but few readers experience any confusion when they see this headline. To them, the frontier analogy says simply that makers, marketers, and users of Velcro stand on the edge of exciting possibilities. Velcro is a frontier because Velcro has thousands of still-to-be-imagined uses. No normal reader, if one defines "normal reader" as a person who is not a Western American historian, would even notice the peculiar implications of the analogy. For most Americans in the twentieth century, the term "frontier" is perfectly clear, reliable, and simple in its meanings.

"Frontier," the historian David Wrobel writes, "has become a metaphor for promise, progress, and ingenuity."[2] And yet, despite the accuracy of this summation, the relation between the frontier and the American mind is not a simple one. Clear and predictable on most occasions, the idea of the frontier is still capable of sudden twists and shifts of meaning, meanings considerably more interesting than the conventional and familiar definition of the frontier as a zone of open opportunity.

Conventional thinking is at its most powerful, however, in twentieth-century reconstructions of the nineteenth-century experience of westward expansion, reconstructions quite explicitly designed for sale. To see this commercialized vision of the Old Frontier in concrete, three-dimensional form, the best place to go is Disneyland in Anaheim, California. When they enter Frontierland, visitors might ask Disneyland employees for directions, but they do not have to ask for a definition of the frontier. The frontier, every tourist knows, was the edge of Anglo-American settlement, the place where white Americans struggled to master the continent. This frontier, as everything in Frontierland confirms, was populated by a colorful and romantic cast of characters—mountain men, cowboys, prospectors, pioneer wives, saloon girls, sheriffs, and outlaws. Tepees, log cabins, and false-front stores were the preferred architecture of the frontier; coonskin caps, cowboy hats, bandannas, buckskin shirts and leggings, moccasins, boots, and an occasional sunbonnet or calico dress constituted frontier fashion; canoes, keelboats, steamboats, saddle horses, covered wagons, and stagecoaches gave Americans the means to conquer the rivers, mountains, deserts, plains, and other wide-open spaces of the frontier; firearms, whether long rifles or six-shooters, were everywhere and in frequent use. These images are very well understood. Tourists do not need any assistance in defining Frontierland.

And yet, even in the tightly controlled world of Disneyland, the idea of the frontier has encountered complications. At the Golden Horseshoe, Frontierland's saloon, every show once had a "spontaneous" gunfight in which Black Bart and Sheriff Lucky blazed away at each other. In 1958, as a reporter for the *Saturday Evening Post* watched, the gunfight underwent some slippage at the joint that connects fantasy to reality: "As the sheriff advanced toward the wounded bandit," the writer said, "a tow-headed five-year-old, wearing a cowboy suit and holding a cap pistol, came running from the crowd," asking earnestly, "'Can I finish him off, sheriff, can I?'" The sheriff consented, and everyone fired.

> Black Bart shuddered, then lay deathly still.
> The lad took one look, dropped his gun and fled, screaming, "Mommy, mommy! I didn't mean to! I didn't mean to!"

Scholars with a penchant for interpreting signs, symbols, and signifiers could go to town with this incident, pondering the way in which the appeal to "mommy" follows hard and fast on the attempted initiation into the manly sport of gunplay. But my own attention fixes on the line, "I didn't mean to!" Since the child wanted to kill Black Bart, and, with an impressive deference to authority, asked the sheriff for permission to kill him, why would he then make the claim, "I didn't mean to"? His worries of intention and outcome were, in any case, soon ended: "His tears stopped a moment later, however, when he turned and saw Black Bart and Sheriff Lucky walking into the Golden Horseshoe to get ready for their next performance."[3] Rather than feeling soothed, another sort of child might at that moment have conceived a long-range ambition to kill *both* Black Bart and Sheriff Lucky for their complicity in tricking him.

In the twentieth century, as this boy learned, the image of the frontier balances precariously between too much reality and too little. Properly screened and edited, the doings of the Old Frontier are quite a bit of fun. But when encounters with death, or injury, or conflict, or loss become unexpectedly convincing and compelling, then fun can make an abrupt departure, while emotions considerably more troubling take its place.

The outlaw-killing lad was not the only child encountering the limits of

Frontierland's fun, not the only one to stumble in the uncertain turf along the border between the imagined and the actual. As the *Saturday Evening Post* writer described it, one "seven-year-old boy was certain he could tell the real from the unreal."

> As they jogged along on the burro ride, the leathery mule-skinner warned, "Look out for them thar cactus plants. Them needles is mighty sharp."
>
> The skeptical boy leaned over and took a swipe at the cactus. On the way to the first-aid station, he decided all was not fantasy at Disneyland. The management has since moved the cactus out of reach.[4]

Moving the cactus—finding the place where its thorns could *look* sharp and scary but not *be* sharp and scary—can serve as a fine representation of the whole process of getting authenticity into the proper adjustment at Frontierland. When too many surprised innocents made visits to the first-aid stand, the frontier was clearly out of alignment, and a repositioning was in order.

And yet, in other parts of Frontierland's turf, wounds and injuries were a taken-for-granted dimension of frontier life. At Tom Sawyer's Island, as the *Saturday Evening Post* writer put it, kids "can fire air-operated, bulletless rifles at the plastic Indians."[5] A writer for the *Reader's Digest* described the same opportunity in 1960: "From the top of a log fort you can sight in with guns on a forest in which Indians lurk. The guns don't fire bullets—they're hydraulically operated—but the recoil is so realistic that you'd never guess they aren't the genuine article."[6]

The Indians of this frontier were not, however, the sort to hold a grudge. Visitors could fire away at the Indians and then move on to a voyage in "Indian canoes paddled by real Indians."[7] "Realness" was not, in this case, an easy matter to arrange. "Wanting authentic Native Americans to paddle canoes full of guests around the rivers of the theme area, Disneyland recruited employees from southwestern tribes," the historian John Findlay writes in his book *Magic Lands*. "These Indians, of course, came from the desert rather than a riverine or lakes environment, so they had to be taught how to paddle canoes by white employees of the park who had learned the skill at summer camp."[8]

Over the decades, life at Frontierland has become, if anything, more confusing for those rare individuals who stop and think about what they are seeing. There is, for instance, the question of the frontier's geographical location. On one side of a path, a roller coaster rushes through a southwestern mesa, carved into a mine. On the other side of the path, the great river, with its stately steamboat, rolls by. Where is the frontier? Evidently where New Mexico borders on the Mississippi River, where western gold and silver miners load their ore directly onto steamboats heading to New Orleans.

In recent times, even the ritualized violence betwen whites and Indians has become a matter of some awkwardness. On the various rides along the Rivers of America, one passes a settler's cabin, wildly in flames. In my childhood, the guides announced that the cabin was on fire because Indians had attacked it. In current times, the cabin is just on fire, usually without commentary or blame. At the further reaches of cultural change lies the recent experience of an acquaintance: the guide told his group that the cabin was on fire because the settler had been ecologically and environmentally careless.[9]

Consider, as well, the curious politics of the shooting gallery encountered at the entrance to Frontierland. Visitors can take firearm in hand and shoot at a variety of targets—including a railroad train, winding its way through a sculpted landscape. But if you are shooting at a railroad train, then *who*—in this frontier role-play—*are you*? Which side are you on? If you are firing on the train, then you seem to be either a hostile Indian or a murderous and larcenous outlaw. What is going on here? Is the visitor receiving an invitation to play with point of view, to reconsider the whole question of the identity and interests of good guys and bad guys, champions of progress and opponents of progress? Or is this casting of the railroad as target simply the product of Disneyland's designers working under the mandate to create a scene chock-full of the shapes and forms that will say "frontier," with the assumption that any visitor so stimulated visually will fall into step with the mythic patterns of frontier life, pick up a gun, and blast away at whatever is in sight?

If professional Western American historians find themselves conceptually without anchor when they visit Frontierland, the reason is clear: with the possible exception of the suggestion that environmental carelessness produced the settler's cabin fire, the work of academic historians has had virtually no impact either on Disneyland's vision of the frontier or on the thinking of Disneyland's visitors. That cheerful and complete indifference to the work of frontier historians may, in truth, be the secret of the place's success.

The Fight for the Frontier in the History Department

In recent years, academic historians have given the idea of the frontier a pretty rough overhauling. Nicknamed the "f-word" and pummeled for its ethnocentrism and vagueness, the term has from time to time landed on the ropes, perilously close to conceding the match. But a determined group of trainers and handlers has always trooped out to the rescue, braced up the frontier, and gotten it back on its feet for the next round.

The academic boxing match centers on this question: how well does the concept of the frontier perform the task of describing, explaining, and encapsulating the story of the colonization of North America? "Miserably," answers one group of historians, of which I happen to be a member.[10] "Pretty well," responds a different set of historians, "if you make a few adjustments and realignments in its definition."

The case for the frailty of the "f-word" is an easy one to make. First, built into the idea is an inflexible point of view. For the term to have clear meaning, historians have had to hand their point of view over to the custody of English-speaking white people. In its clearest and most concrete meaning, as Richard White has said, the frontier was where white people got scarce—or, with a friendly amendment, the frontier was where white people got *scared* because they were scarce. This perspective has certainly been an important psychological reality in American history, and it is a psychological reality well worth study. But using the frontier as an analytic concept puts the historian at risk of adopting the point of view of only one of the contesting groups. Moreover, the frontier came with two sides, the Anglo-American side and the one labeled "the other side of the frontier." Jammed into the second category were Indians of all tribes (often tribes that fought against each other as well as against Anglo Americans), long-term Hispano settlers, and more recent Mexican immigrants. In lived reality, the people on this "other side of the frontier" did not form anything remotely resembling a united team or a homogeneous society. Conceptually, neither "side" of the frontier offered much in the way of accommodations for Asian Americans, who came from the "wrong" direction, or for African Americans, participants in the westward movement who encountered a full measure of restrictions and exclusions. Trying to grasp the enormous human complexity of the American West is not easy under any circumstances, and the effort to reduce a tangle of many-sided encounters to a world defined by a frontier line only makes a tough task even tougher.

Second, the idea of the frontier runs almost entirely on an east-to-west track. Indeed, to most of its users, the term "frontier" has been a synonym for the American nation's westward movement. Can such a term do justice to the prior presence of Indian people, to the northward movement of Spanish-speaking people, or the eastward movement of Asians? The east-to-west movement of Anglo Americans and African Americans is enormously important, but so are these movements of other people. Try to wrap the term "frontier" around all these movements, and the poor idea stretches to the point of snapping.

Third, it is nearly impossible to define either the beginning or the ending of a frontier. If one cannot define the beginning or ending of a condition, it is not going to be easy to say when that condition is present and when it is *not* present. Return, for instance, to Frederick Jackson Turner's definition of a frontier, borrowed from the Census Department, as a place where the population numbers fewer than two people per square mile. Then think of a mining rush—where, as soon as the news of the gold or silver gets out, the population instantly exceeds two people per square mile, with enough people to form a camp or a town. By Turner's definition, then, one would have to declare the mining frontier closed virtually the moment it opened.

Other scholars have offered more enterprising, and certainly more colorful, definitions of the closing of the frontier. One of the best comes from the historian Paula Petrik, who studied prostitutes in Helena, Montana. In the early years of Helena, Petrik reports, the prostitutes tended to be their own employers. They were able to hold on to the rewards of their labors, and some of them saved significant amounts of money, owned real estate, and lent money at interest. But then, as the frontier phase passed, men took control of the prostitutes and their earnings. This, I thought when I first heard Petrik's evidence and argument, is the most interesting marker of the end of the frontier I am ever going to hear: the frontier ends when the pimps come to town.[11]

My own entry in the "closing" competition rests on the popularization of tourism and the quaintness of the folk. When Indian war dances became tourist spectacles, when the formerly scorned customs of the Chinese drew tourists to Chinatown, when former out-groups found that characteristics that once earned them disapproval could now earn them a living, when fearful, life-threatening deserts became charming patterns of color and light, the war was over and the frontier could be considered closed, even museumized. But this nomination comes with its own fatal flaw. Let the car break down in the desert, or let the Indians file a lawsuit to reassert an old land claim, and the quaint appeal of nature and native can abruptly vanish. The frontier is suddenly reopened, and the whole question of beginnings and endings becomes unsettled again.

Fourth, a presumption of innocence and exceptionalism is interwoven with the roots of frontier history, as Americans have understood it. The contrast becomes clearest when one thinks of a nation like South Africa.

Europeans forcibly took South Africa from the natives, everyone under-stands, and the residents still struggle with the consequences. But the idea of the frontier permits the United States to make an appeal to innocence and exceptionalism: while South Africa underwent an invasion and a con-quest, the United States had an expanding frontier of democracy, oppor-tunity, and equality.

The term "frontier" blurs the fact of conquest and throws a veil over the similarities between the story of American westward expansion and the planetary story of the expansion of European empires. Whatever meanings historians give the term, in popular culture it carries a persistently happy affect, a tone of adventure, heroism, and even fun very much in contrast with the tough, complicated, and sometimes bloody and brutal realities of conquest. Under these conditions, the word "frontier" uses historians be-fore historians can use it.

Fifth, an unthinking reliance on the idea of the frontier almost ruined Western American history. For too many years, Western historians let Frederick Jackson Turner do most of their thinking for them. By accept-ing many of Turner's boundaries, Western historians drastically narrowed the scope of their field. Consider, for instance, the number of important economic activities ignored by conventional frontier historians. Scholars wrote voluminously about the mining frontier and the cattle frontier, but the logging frontier, the fishing frontier, the tourism-promoting frontier, the investing-in-real-estate-and-mortgages frontier, and the labor-contracting frontier remained very much understudied. Grain-based agriculture domi-nated the category of the farming frontier; no book appeared under the title *The Vegetable Frontier* or *The Fruit Frontier*. Few of the important eco-nomic enterprises resting on women's labor registered in the occupational frontier model: *The Poultry Frontier, The Laundry Frontier, The Sewing Fron-tier, The Boardinghouse Frontier,* and *The Sexual Services Frontier* all await their authors.[12] Similarly, since conventional frontier historians rigorously observed the 1890 Turnerian deadline for the closing, enterprises that started late—the copper, coal, petroleum, moviemaking, skiing, atomic-weapons-developing, and defense-spending frontiers—could not qualify for study.

The field of Western American history could never achieve its full vitality and range of subjects unless the crucial term "frontier" underwent critical reexamination. To some scholars, critical reexamination could lead to rehabilitation, with a more carefully thought-out, more inclusive, less ethnocentric definition of the term. In 1962 the historian Jack Forbes began a campaign to define the frontier "as an *inter-group contact situation*," "an instance of dynamic interaction between human beings," involving "such processes as acculturation, assimilation, miscegenation, race prejudice, conquest, imperialism, and colonialism."[13]

In a collection of essays comparing colonization in North America and southern Africa, published in 1981, the historians Howard Lamar and Leonard Thompson joined the campaign for a transformed definition of the frontier, "not as a boundary or line, but a territory or zone of interpenetration between two previously distinct societies." What marked the beginning or the ending of such a condition of interpenetration? "The frontier 'opens' in a given zone when the first representatives of the intrusive society arrive," Lamar and Thompson explained; "it 'closes' when a single political authority has established hegemony over the zone."[14]

In the most recent campaigns to brace up the idea of the frontier, the historians William Cronon, George Miles, and Jay Gitlin offer a six-part definition of the frontier process: species shifting, market making, land taking, boundary setting, state forming, and self shaping.[15] Stephen Aron argues for what he calls "the Greater Western History," a reconceived model of the westward movement with more recognition of cultural and moral complexity.[16]

In the meantime, while some historians pressed the definition of the frontier in the direction of cultural complexity, a considerably better publicized set of writers pushed their definition in the opposite direction entirely. Returning to Turner's quantitative approach and defining the frontier as a place where the population numbers between two and six people per square mile, the urban planner Frank Popper declared that "the frontier survives to this day as a distinct geographical region—a large remote land area beyond the farthest settlement—across huge stretches of the United States." The Turnerian obituaries were premature, Popper felt.

"The frontier never died and shows no signs of dying."[17] Following Popper's model, the journalist Dayton Duncan traveled the areas with fewer than two people per square mile and described them in *Miles from Nowhere*. "In 1990," Duncan wrote, "on the centennial of the 'closing of the frontier,' the census found 132 counties within fifteen Western states in the Lower 48 that still had fewer than two people per square mile," with this land composing "13 percent of the nation's contiguous landmass."[18]

While it was the clearest heir to the Turnerian definition, the Popper-and-Duncan frontier had nothing to do with the conventional vision of the frontier as a place of open opportunity and sudden growth; on the contrary, their frontier was still around because certain areas of the United States had proven so resistant to conventional American settlement that the population had never grown much, or had, over the twentieth century, shrunk. But Frank Popper had by no means won the definitional war. In the winter of 1993, the title of a newly published book on western American cities—*The Metropolitan Frontier: Cities in the Modern American West*—cheerfully ignored Popper and again defined the frontier as an area of open opportunity and rapid population growth.[19]

In the late twentieth century, the scholarly tug-of-war over the term "frontier" was a long way from resolution. As Turner had said in 1893, the term is "an elastic one, and for our purposes does not need sharp definition." One hundred years later, despite earnest scholarly efforts to define the frontier, "elasticity" and confused meaning formed its one constant characteristic.

To a determined opponent of the f-word, these efforts at definitional clarity have not added up to much. Is sparse population truly the only characteristic of a frontier that "counts"? If one rejects the quantitative definition and turns to the cultural, doesn't the "cultural competition" definition of a frontier in fact describe the pattern of human relations everywhere on the planet? How could one tell the difference between the contested group relations of a frontier and the contested group relations of, say, a late-twentieth-century American city? Is it, in truth, any easier to locate a moment of clearly "established hegemony" than it was to locate any of the other conclusions to the frontier? Can a mega-process that includes everything from species shifting to self defining really leave any coherence in the word "frontier"? Can the Greater Western History, still traveling on an east-to-west track, do justice to the prior presence of Indians and Hispanics?

These definitions leave me discontented, but I announce here a breakthrough in my thinking about these matters: satisfying *my* standards may not be the goal here. What is considerably more important than my definitional contentment is that a number of talented scholars—Walter Nugent, William Cronon, John Mack Faragher, Stephen Aron, Gregory Nobles, James Merrell, and Daniel Usner, to name a few—are doing important and influential work under this label. I continue to believe that all scholars would be well advised to use the term "frontier" with great caution, to take the five objections summarized here as a kind of "surgeon general's warning" on the hazards of the unthinking use of the word. And yet it may not matter a great deal whether these scholars call their territory "conquest studies," "colonization studies," "expansion-of-the-world-market studies," "zone-of-cultural-interaction studies," or "frontier studies." In spirit and style, frontier history has become much more dynamic and inclusive, and that fact outweighs the problem of terminology.

Some of my newfound flexibility on this subject comes, I confess, from the personal experience of having to teach the first half of the American history survey. I am a regular hand on the second half of the survey, but spring 1993 was my first round on the pre-1865 course. Repeatedly during the term, in front of a hundred students, I would encounter a dilemma of expression. I would want to refer to the white people living at the edge of colonial Pennsylvanian settlement, or to refer to the settlers living with Daniel Boone in Kentucky. I would, in other words, pretty clearly want to say the f-word. But I had a public position to uphold, and I would *not* say the f-word. The result was that I sometimes took a sentence or two to say what others could say with one adjective or noun. I would not be surprised if some of the students thought that I was troubled with a peculiar speech impediment that came upon me whenever English colonists or Anglo Americans ventured into the interior.

These episodes gave me unexpected empathy with the addicted users of the word "frontier," and that empathy provides the bedrock explanation behind the truce of terminology I now offer. But the other part of the explanation lies in a recognition of the shared hopelessness, powerlessness, and defeatedness of our positions. Scholars who are holding on to the use of the word "frontier" and scholars who have rejected it hold one thing in common: the public is paying absolutely no attention to either of us. Look wherever you like—Frontierland, newspaper headlines, book titles, politicians' speeches, promotional literature for the National Aeronautics and Space Administration—and it is perfectly evident that the public has a very clear understanding of the word "frontier," and that understanding has no relation at all to the definitional struggling of contemporary historians.

Consider, for instance, the license plates of Alaska. Alaska is a state with an enormous amount of unpopulated land, but, by the same token, it is a state where the vast majority of the people live, not outdoors in nature, but in cities. In that very urbanized state, each automobile sports a license plate with the words, "Alaska: The Last Frontier." Not a single one of the drivers, I am willing to bet, understands this to mean, "Alaska: The Last Zone of Cultural Interpenetration and Contested Hegemony."

As this and thousands of other examples show, the popular understanding of the word "frontier" and the scholarly effort to reckon with the complex history of cultural encounters in colonization share almost no common ground, despite their shared roots in the thinking of the nineteenth century. Indeed, my own fine-tuned sensitivity to the problems of the word "frontier" has been completely drowned out in this discourse. To any newspaper reporter or reader, the fact that I write about the American West translates instantly into the fact that I write about the frontier. As one of many examples, consider the headline of a story in the *New York Times* "Week in Review" a few years ago: "Among Historians," the headline read, "the Old Frontier Is Turning Nastier with Each Revision."[20] The word "nastier" struck me as unfortunate, but I was even more astonished by the uninvited appearance of the word "frontier." Even if I thought I was telling the rich and complicated story of a region set free of old definitions, it was going to go on the public record as the story of "the Old Frontier."

An unexpected comfort, however, descends on the soul with the recognition that no one is paying any attention to the complex shadings of academic debate. The relief from responsibility is considerable. And that is the spirit, one of cheerful despair, in which I turn to the question, "What are the habits of mind that cluster around the word 'frontier' in late-twentieth-century popular culture?"

Presidential Politics on the Frontier

Presidents and presidential candidates are a distinct minority in the American population. And yet their circumstances render them useful as case studies in popular attitudes. In the last half of the twentieth century, electoral politics makes a presidential candidate into the navigational equivalent of a bat, sending off signals, reading the signals as they bounce back, and attempting to set a course based on what these signals reveal. When presidential candidates and presidents put the frontier analogy to use, there is a broader lesson available on the persuasive powers given to that analogy by particular styles of presentation at particular times.

On July 15, 1960, in Los Angeles, California, John F. Kennedy faced "west on what was once the last frontier" and accepted the Democratic presidential nomination. In mid-speech he retold the familiar Turnerian story of westward expansion:

> From the lands that stretch three thousand miles behind me, the
> pioneers of old gave up their safety, their comfort, and sometimes
> their lives to build a new world here in the West. . . . They were
> determined to make that new world strong and free, to overcome
> its hazards and its hardships, to conquer the enemies that threatened
> from within and without.

These "enemies" were, presumably, a combination of natural forces, natives, and cautious naysayers who resisted the currents of Manifest Destiny. The success of John F. Kennedy's rhetoric rested not only on oratorical skill but also on historical timing: he gave this speech before the rise of environmentalism, the resurgence of Indian activism, and the onset of widespread queasiness over American overseas imperialism shifted the terrain of national opinion regarding those "enemies that threatened from within and without."[21] Kennedy was free to offer an image of the New Frontier, premised on the assumption that the campaigns of the Old Frontier had been successful, and morally justified.

Like Turner, most Americans in Kennedy's audience assumed that the frontier had closed in the nineteenth century.[22] "Today," Kennedy proclaimed, "some would say that those struggles are all over—that all the horizons have been explored, that all the battles have been won, that there is no longer an American frontier." That notion, however, could no longer stand: "For the problems are not all solved and the battles are not all won—and we stand today on the edge of a New Frontier—the frontier of the 1960s—a frontier of unknown opportunities and perils—a frontier of unfulfilled hopes and threats." Here was an image of the frontier that seemed composed of equal parts of Buffalo Bill Cody and Frederick Jackson Turner: half a frontier of violence and inverted conquest, in which innocent Americans defended themselves against the attacks of savages, and half a frontier of peaceful, pastoral Americans seeking a better world. "I tell you," Kennedy declared, "the New Frontier is here, whether we seek it or not."

> Beyond that frontier are the uncharted areas of science and space, unsolved problems of peace and war, unconquered pockets of ignorance and prejudice, unanswered questions of poverty and surplus. It would be easier to shrink back from that frontier. . . . But I believe the times demand invention, innovation, imagination, decision. I am asking you to be new pioneers on that New Frontier.

And then, with the topic of foreign affairs, the analogy made a clear shift toward the violent frontier of Cody:

> For the harsh facts of the matter are that we stand on this frontier at a turning point in history. We must prove all over again whether this nation—or any nation so conceived—can long endure; whether our society . . . can compete with the single-minded advance of the Communist system.

On this "race for mastery of the sky and the rain, the ocean and the tides, the far side of space and the inside of men's minds" hinged the prospects of the New Frontier.[23] Drawn from both Cody and Turner, the 1890s vision of the frontier as the triumphant but demanding crusade of the American people made a nearly perfect match with the 1960s search for language to direct and motivate the American public in the midst of the Cold War.

Twenty years later, one might expect a few things to have changed in the usefulness of the frontier analogy. Indian people were active in pressing their rights; the environmental price of conquest was visible and publicized; the imposition of American will by force had stumbled in Vietnam. But none of this discouraged President Ronald Reagan. The imagery of pioneers and frontiers echoed through his speeches and through his "lifestyle," as he vacationed on the "ranch" in Southern California, with horse and cowboy hat in conspicuous display. In a memorable conflation of Washington, D.C., and the West, the Secret Service named the riding trails after streets in Washington, D.C., and code-named the president "Rawhide." Thus, the phrase "Rawhide entering Pennsylvania Avenue" meant that the president was "entering the main trail" at his ranch. "Rawhide" rode down "Pennsylvania Avenue" with some frequency. "There is nothing better for the inside of a man," Reagan was fond of saying, "than the outside of a horse."[24]

On the Fourth of July, 1982, greeting the return of the space shuttle to Edwards Air Force Base, Reagan gave his fullest tribute to Turnerian frontier history. "The conquest of new frontiers for the betterment of our homes and families," he said, "is a crucial part of our national character." Like Kennedy, Reagan parted from Turner to affirm the openness of America's frontiers: "There are those who thought the closing of the Western frontier marked an end to America's greatest period of vitality. Yet we're crossing new frontiers every day." With the specter of a closed frontier disposed of, Reagan returned to the Turnerian terms of basic American character; the space shuttle's astronauts "reaffirm to all of us that as long as there are frontiers to be explored and conquered, Americans will lead the way."[25]

In his second inaugural address, Reagan pitched into a celebration of westward expansion:

> [T]he men of the Alamo call out encouragement to each other; a settler pushes west and sings his song, and the song echoes out forever and fills the unknowing air.
>
> It is the American sound: It is hopeful, bighearted, idealistic— daring, decent and fair. That's our heritage, that's our song. We sing it still. For all our problems, we are together as of old.[26]

Twenty-five years after Kennedy's New Frontier, could such rhetoric still work? The columnist William Safire felt that it certainly did. The song of the settler, Safire thought, was "a lovely metaphor, and enabled [the President] to use the half-dozen adjectives that describe his vision of America: 'hopeful, bighearted, idealistic—daring, decent and fair.'"[27] In his State of the Union speech two weeks later, Reagan stuck with the frontier, celebrating "a revolution carrying us to new heights of progress by pushing back frontiers of space and knowledge."[28]

And yet an embrace of the frontier metaphor was no guarantee of electoral success. In 1988, running for the Democratic presidential nomination, Massachusetts Governor Michael Dukakis adopted the slogan "The Next American Frontier," and repeated it assiduously in his stump speech.[29] He began with the requisite quotation from John F. Kennedy on the New Frontier. This race in 1988, Dukakis said, "must not be about succumbing to shrunken ambitions. It must be about building the future we want, and conquering the next American frontier." What was this frontier? Here rhetorical force faded, as Dukakis simply proceeded through a catalogue:

> [T]he next American frontier is a vibrant, growing economy that provides good jobs at good wages for every citizen in the land. . . .

> The next American frontier is in the marketplace of our international competition. . . .

> The next American frontier is the American mind. . . .

> The next American frontier is the millions of Americans who have been left behind. . . .

> The next American frontier is the health of our people. . . .

> . . . the next American frontier [is] in the democratic leaders of Central and Latin America who want to work with us for peace and economic development.[30]

Something, it seems clear, was not working in this speech; the energy that Reagan could pull out of the frontier metaphor was simply not available to Dukakis. He could not go beyond a formulation of equivalence: "frontier" equals "social or political issue." For reasons one can only guess at, Dukakis would not carry through on the analogy. He would not say, "The next American frontier is in the marketplace of our international competition, and we shall fight the barriers that obstruct American trade just as our pioneer ancestors fought the wilderness and the Indians." The Democratic presidential candidate in 1960 could follow the frontier analogy all the way up to an attack on "enemies that threatened from within and without"; the Democratic presidential candidate in 1988 showed a perfectly understandable reluctance to go all the way. Dukakis could only repeat his mantra of diminished power, "the next American frontier," and hope for the best.

The Headline Frontier

The headlines in 1986 looked as if they had been co-authored by Frederick Jackson Turner and the director of the 1890 census:

> Frontier's Fate Still Uncertain
> Frontier Still Has a Chance for Survival
> Frontier Verges on Collapse
> Time Runs Out for Frontier
> Frontier Shuts Down
> Too Late for Frontier
> Frontier Throws in the Towel
> Frontier Files for Bankruptcy
> Politics Killed Frontier
> Frontier Legacy Lives [31]

The entity in question was Frontier Airlines, struggling for financial survival. For readers in Colorado in 1986, the fate of the airline was a subject of some anxiety; the ironic historical resonance of these headlines offered little in the way of consolation or diversion.

Seldom recognized for its ironic implications, the word "frontier" appears frequently in headlines. To serve their function, headlines have to convey some trustworthy clue to the contents of the story they introduce. But headlines are very short; they are virtually a freeze-dried form of communication. Thus, their writers tap out their message in a kind of code. In the necessary economy of the headline, the writers go in search of words that will convey big meanings. They have, under those circumstances, little interest in treacherous words, words that stand a chance of betraying their users.

Headline writers are, predictably, heavy users of the words "frontier" and "pioneer." They trust those words, and the words repay that trust. They are words that carry the master key to the reader's mind; with that key, they can slip into the mind and deposit their meanings before anyone quite knows they are there.

To assemble a set of artifacts demonstrating the persistent and widespread power of these words, I looked at roughly four thousand headlines, from 1988 through the first half of 1993, that made use of "frontier" and "pioneer." The first time through, I made a strategic error, and simply looked to see how silly these references were. This was an easy exercise, because many of the usages are indeed goofy. But at the end of the exercise, I had to realize that simply chuckling over these phrases was not accomplishing much for the cause of understanding.

The next time, then, I tried to find the patterns in the usage of these words. What seems to be going on in people's minds in the late twentieth century when they call someone a pioneer or refer to an activity or an enterprise as a frontier? Answering this question can illuminate even the sillier usages, showing just how far from historical reality this historical reference has strayed. This exercise works best if the reader picks a nineteenth-century pioneer and then imagines how that pioneer might respond to his or her twentieth-century descendants. Or one might think only of Frederick Jackson Turner and imagine his response to what the twentieth century has done to his favorite term and his favorite people.

Let us begin on the comparatively neutral frontier of food. "Eating to Heal: The New Frontiers," the *New York Times* announced in 1990. Apparently fighting on the wrong side of this frontier was the "Cookie Pioneer," "creator of the fortune cookie folding machine and a line of risqué fortune cookies." The Cookie Pioneer may have held only a superficial kinship to the Cinnamon Roll Pioneers, but all of these pioneers could have joined forces with the Fast Food Pioneer and the Pioneer of the

Snack Food Industry to defend their turf against the insinuations of the Natural Foods Pioneer, the Vegetarian Pioneer, and the Pioneer of the Edible Landscape. Occupying less contested territory were the Pasta Pioneers, the Potato Pioneer, and the Microwave Popcorn Pioneer, and surely the most memorable of the food pioneers—the Pioneer of the South Philadelphia Hoagie.[32]

As striking as the food pioneers are the "lifestyle pioneers": the Passionate Pioneer of Fitness Franchising (the woman who founded Jazzercise Inc.); the Surfing Pioneer ("he pioneered a whole way of surfing for thousands"); the Psychedelic Pioneer; the New Age Pioneer; the Sex-Change Pioneer; the Porn Pioneer; the Pioneer in the Crack Business; and the Peekaboo Pioneer, the founder of Frederick's of Hollywood. Frederick's pioneering work did not exhaust the possibilities of the underwear frontier: "Underwear Pioneers Targeting Men," one headline reads, and the story opens with this promising line: "The two designing women who revolutionized the bra industry in the 1970s with the invention of the first jogging bra have turned their talents to men's underwear." On the subject of fabrics and new materials, there is the memorable Polyester Pioneer, as well as a Pioneer of Plastics and a Stainless Steel Cookware Pioneer.[33]

Forced into the discomfort and disorientation of time travel, Frederick Jackson Turner, or any of his contemporaries, would have to experience astonishment at the applications of the word "pioneer" in the late twentieth century, at this implied kinship between overland travelers and marketers of underwear, stainless steel, and hoagies. Of all these contestants, the award for the most unsettling pioneer would have to go to Dr. Louis Irwin Grossman, Pioneer in Root Canal Dentistry. And if there were an award for the twentieth-century pioneer of the product that nineteenth-century pioneers would have had the most occasions to appreciate, then that prize would go to Bernard Castro, described as the Pioneer of the Sleeper-Sofa.[34]

Beneath and beyond the silliness of these references lies a clear set of patterns. The pioneers and frontiers cluster in particular areas and enterprises. Art, music, sports, fashion, commerce, law, and labor activism get their full share of the analogy. Technology holds the biggest cluster: technology of transportation (bicycles, automobiles, helicopters, airplanes, rockets, and spacecraft); technology of communications and information (radio, television, talk shows, CD players, laser discs, computers, software, programming); technology of medicine (heart transplants, plastic surgery, headache treatment, weight reduction, gene therapy); technology of weaponry (rocketry, atomic bombs). Indeed, it is impossible to read all these references to the frontiers of technology without recognizing that the American public has genuinely and completely accepted, ratified, and bought the notion that the American frontiering spirit, sometime in the last century, picked itself up and made a definitive relocation—from territorial expansion to technological and commercial expansion.

In November 1944, as the end of World War II neared, President Franklin Roosevelt asked Vannevar Bush, director of the Office of Scientific Research and Development, to report on the prospects for American science after the war. "New frontiers of the mind," Roosevelt said, "are before us, and if they are pioneered with the same vision, boldness, and drive with which we have waged this war we can create a fuller and more fruitful employment and a fuller and more fruitful life."[35] Called *Science— The Endless Frontier,* Bush's response to Roosevelt's request set the agenda for federally funded science. "It is in keeping with basic United States policy," Bush wrote, "that the Government should foster the opening of new frontiers," and federal investment in science "is the modern way to do it."[36] Casting science as the nation's new frontier, a frontier maintained by hearty federal funding, Vannevar Bush captured and promoted the popular understanding of the frontier's relocation after Turner.

Certainly the space program has provided the best example of this pattern. The promoters of space exploration and development may well qualify as the nation's most committed and persistent users of the frontier analogy. *Pioneering the Space Frontier,* the 1986 Paine commission report on the future of the space program, shows the analogy at its most fervent. The story of the American nation, as imagined by the Paine commissioners, was a triumphant and glorious story of success, with the complex stories of Indian conquest and African American slavery simply ignored and eliminated. "The promise of virgin lands and the opportunity to live in freedom," the commissioners declared, "brought our ancestors to the shores of North America." The frontiers have not closed, and Manifest Destiny has just taken a turn skyward: "Now space technology has freed humankind to move outward from Earth as a species destined to expand to other worlds." The best that the Paine commissioners could offer in recognizing that frontiers might not always be vacant was this memorable line: "As we move outward into the Solar System, we must remain true to our values as Americans: To go forward peacefully and to respect the integrity of planetary bodies and alien life forms, with equality of opportunity for all."[37] If one thinks of the devastation of Indians by disease, alcohol, war, loss of territory, and coercive assimilation, and then places that reality next to the Paine commissioners' pious intentions, one feels some obligation to take up the mission of warning the "alien life forms," to suggest that they keep their many eyes on their wallets when they hear these intentions invoked, especially the line about "equality of opportunity for all."

However this frontier experience plays out for alien life forms, the mental act of equating the frontier of westward expansion with the development of space proved to be an enterprise that ran itself. In the selling of space as "the final frontier," the aerospace industry, the National Aeronautics and Space Administration, presidents, the news media, and the entertainment business collaborated with perfect harmony, with no need for centralized direction or planning, with a seamless match in their methods and goals. The split infinitive was regrettable, but the writers of *Star Trek* came up with the phrase to capture the essential idea brought to mind at the mention of the words "frontier" and "pioneer": "to boldly go where no man has gone before."

Meanwhile, La Frontera

Anglo Americans have fixed their attention on the definition of the frontier drawn from the imaginative reconstruction of the story of the United

States and its westward expansion. But North America has, in fact, had two strong traditions in the use of the term. There is the much more familiar, English, usage of the frontier as the place where white settlers entered a zone of "free" land and opportunity. But there is the much less familiar, but much more realistic, usage of *la frontera,* the borderlands between Mexico and the United States. This is not simply a place where two groups meet; Indian people have been influential players in the complicated pattern of human relations in the area. In the nineteenth century, trade, violence, conquest, and cultural exchange punctuated and shaped life in the borderlands. In the twentieth century, with conflicts over the restriction of immigration, with disputes over water flow and environmental pollution, and with a surge of industrial development and population growth from American-owned businesses (*maquiladoras*) operating in northern Mexico, conditions along the border remain far from tranquil.[38]

In the idea of *la frontera,* there is no illusion of vacancy, of triumphal conclusions, or of simplicity. As the writer Gloria Anzaldúa puts it, the United States–Mexican border is "where the Third World grates up against the first and bleeds."[39] It is a unique place on the planet's surface, a zone where an industrialized nation shares a long land border with a nation much troubled by poverty. "Ambivalence and unrest," Anzaldúa says, "reside there and death is no stranger."[40] Any temptation to romanticize *la frontera*—as a place of cultural syncretism, a place where the Spanish and English languages have learned to cohabit and even merge—runs aground on the bare misery of poverty in the border towns.[41]

The idea of the frontier is extemely well established as cultural common property. If the idea of *la frontera* had anywhere near the standing of the idea of the frontier, we would be well launched toward self-understanding, directed toward a realistic view of this nation's position in the hemisphere and in the world. "The struggle of borders is our reality still," Anzaldúa writes.[42] One can tinker a bit with that line to draw the crucial contrast: "The adventure of frontiers is our fantasy still; the struggle of borders is our reality still."

In truth, this idea of the frontier as border has made some inroads in popular thinking. If you are reading a headline for a news story set outside the United States, there is a chance that the word "frontier" will carry a meaning completely different from its usual one. References to "the Romania-Bulgaria frontier" or to "the Lebanese-Israeli frontier" are quite a different matter from references to the frontier where the pioneer stands on the edge of vacancy and opportunity. These are frontiers in the old, concrete, down-to-earth sense, much closer in meaning to *la frontera:* borders between countries, between peoples, between authorities, sometimes between armies. When "Algeria and Morocco reopen their frontier," or when the nation of Turkey decides it "will close its frontier with Bulgaria," these are references to borders that are full of possibilities for both cooperation and friction, places where the meaning of "opening" and "closing" differs dramatically from what Frederick Jackson Turner and the director of the census meant in the 1890s.[43]

In these references to international borders and boundaries, the word "frontier" takes a firmer hold on reality. In my collection of headlines, the frequent appearance of this definition of frontier caught me by surprise. Perhaps, it began to seem, there is more hope for this word than seemed possible at first; perhaps popular thinking has already dug a sizable channel for thinking about the frontier in a manner quite different from the *Star Trek* mode.

One other pattern of usage, however, struck me as equally surprising: the omnipresence in headlines of African American pioneers. Here, the usage was again closer to the *Star Trek* definition, with pioneers boldly going where no one like them had gone before. Pioneers in civil rights— "Desegregation's Pioneers"—were everywhere, from A. Philip Randolph to Rosa Parks, from Julian Bond to Charlayne Hunter-Gault. The range of African American pioneers covers a great deal of turf: a Pioneer Black Professional Golfer; a Pioneer of Black Pride; the National Football League's Pioneer Black Coach; a Pioneer Black (Theatrical) Producer; a Pioneer Black Announcer; Negro League Pioneers; a Pioneer Black Ivy League Teacher; a Black Radio Pioneer; a Black Foreign Service Pioneer; a Pioneer Black Los Angeles Judge; a Pioneer Black Journalist; a Pioneer in Black Film; and Sidney Poitier, the winner of the "coveted Pioneer Award," bestowed at the Black Oscar Nominees dinner in 1989. As all these headlines suggest, the idea of calling African American people pioneers, as an appropriately complimentary way to refer to their dignity, courage, and determination in traveling where no black person had gone before, has established itself as part of the American cultural vocabulary. When in 1989 Secretary of Health and Human Services Louis Sullivan "told the graduating class of A. Philip Randolph Campus High School in Manhattan that they will become 'pioneers' if they meet the challenges of fighting inequality, racism, and poverty in the 21st century," Sullivan was employing the term in its standard usage.[44]

This usage was so well understood that it gave rise to one of the few cases where a person interviewed in a newspaper article actually engaged and questioned the meaning of the term "pioneer," and its application to him. "National League President Plays Down 'Pioneer' Talk," the headline read. The opening sentence explained, "National League President Bill White says he's getting tired of people referring to him as a black pioneer. . . . 'I'm not a pioneer,' White said. 'Jackie [Robinson] was the pioneer.'"[45] To Bill White, "pioneer" was the term reserved for the unusually courageous person who went first, and the one who faced the worst and the most intense opposition and resistance.

The African American applications of the pioneer analogy caught me completely by surprise. They took the ground out from under any remaining inclination I might have had simply to mock the analogy. The lesson of these references is this: the whole package of frontier and pioneer imagery has ended up as widely dispersed intellectual property. One could argue, as I probably at other times *would* have argued, that African Americans would be well advised to keep their distance from the metaphors and analogies of conquest and colonialism, that there are other, and better, ways to say that someone was a person of principle, innovation, and determination without calling him or her a pioneer. Even though they have been significant participants in the westward movement and in the life of the American West in the twentieth century, African Americans barely figured in the traditional tellings of frontier history; the history of pioneer-ing Americans was for far too long a segregated, "whites-only" subject matter.[46] The image of the heroic pioneer was in many ways a vehicle of racial subordination, exalting the triumph of whites over Indians. Jackie Robinson, A. Philip Randolph, and Rosa Parks were people of great courage and spirit, and getting them entangled in the whole inherited myth of Manifest Destiny, nationalistic cheerleading, and justifications for conquest does not seem to be the best way to honor them.

But it is a bit too late to avoid that entangling. Greatly troubled by the problem of violence inflicted by blacks against blacks, Rev. Jesse Jackson pled with people to "Stop the violence!" The campaign to end the vio-lence, he said, is "the new frontier of the civil rights movement."[47] Logic and history say that the frontier was, in fact, a place where violence served the causes of racial subordination, but a more powerful emotional under-standing says that the frontier is where people of courage have gone to take a stand for the right and the good. For people of a wide range of ethnici-ties, when it comes to the idea of the frontier, logic and history yield to the much greater power of inherited image.

This is the curious conclusion that these headlines forced upon me: a positive image of the frontier and the pioneer is now implanted in nearly everyone's mind. It would not surprise me to see headlines referring to an American Indian lawyer as "a pioneer in the assertion of Indian legal rights," "pushing forward the frontier of tribal sovereignty"—even though it was the historical pioneers who assaulted those rights, even though it was the pioneers' historical frontier that charged head-on into tribal sover-eignty. And yet Indian people have adopted any number of items intro-duced by whites. They wear cowboy hats, drive pickup trucks and auto-mobiles, shop in supermarkets, study constitutional law in law schools, and remain Indian. In all sorts of ways, Indian people put Anglo-American ar-tifacts, mental and physical, to use for Indian purposes. There is no very convincing argument for saying they must put a stop to their adopting and incorporating when it comes to the idea of the frontier and the image of the pioneer.

The historian Arthur Schlesinger, Jr., and many others have recently lamented "the disuniting of America" through the expansion of multicultural history.[48] We hear frequent expressions of nostalgia for an imagined era of unity, before an emphasis on race, class, and gender divided Americans into contesting units and interests. Reading several thousand headlines about pioneers and frontiers, however, convinced me that matters are by no means as disunited as the lamenters think. When African Americans turn comfortably to the image of the pioneer, then the idea of the frontier and the pioneer have clearly become a kind of multicultural common property, a joint-stock company of the imagination. As encounters with scholars from other countries usually demonstrate, this is not just multicultural, this is international. People from the Philippines, people from Senegal, people from Thailand, people with plenty of reasons to resent the frontier and cowboy diplomacy inflicted on their nations by our nation: many of them nonetheless grew up watching western movies and yearning for life on the Old Frontier and the open range.[49]

As a mental artifact, the frontier has demonstrated an astonishing stickiness and persistence. It is virtually the flypaper of our mental world; it attaches itself to everything—healthful diets, space shuttles, civil rights campaigns, heart transplants, industrial product development, musical innovations. Packed full of nonsense and goofiness, jammed with nationalistic self-congratulation and toxic ethnocentrism, the image of the frontier is nonetheless universally recognized, and laden with positive associations. Whether or not it suits my preference, the concept works as a cultural glue—a mental and emotional fastener that, in some very curious and unexpected ways, works to hold us together.

The frontier of an expanding and confident nation; the frontier of cultural interpenetration; the frontier of contracting rural settlement; the frontier of science, technology, and space; the frontier of civil rights where black pioneers ventured and persevered; the frontiers between nations in Europe, Asia, and Africa; *la frontera* of the Rio Grande and the deserts of the southwestern United States and northern Mexico: somewhere in this weird hodgepodge of frontier and pioneer imagery lie important lessons about the American identity, sense of history, and direction for the future. Standing in the way of a full reckoning with those lessons, however, is this fact: in the late *twentieth* century, the scholarly understanding formed in the late *nineteenth* century still governs most of the public rhetorical uses of the word "frontier"; the vision of Frederick Jackson Turner still governs the common and conventional understandings of the term. If the movement of ideas from frontier historians to popular culture maintains its velocity, sometime in the next century we might expect the popular usage of the word to begin to reckon with the complexity of the westward movement and its consequences. Somewhere in the mid-2000s the term might make a crucial shift, toward the reality of *la frontera* and away from the fantasy of the frontier. And that shift in meaning, *if* it occurs, will mark a great change in this nation's understanding of its own origins.

Notes

I would like to thank Kim Gruenwald, Stephen Sturgeon, and Jon Coleman for their help in following the trail of the frontier. I would also like to thank my colleague Mark Pittenger, whose book *American Socialists and Evolutionary Thought, 1870–1920* (Madison: University of Wisconsin Press, 1993) showed me how to think about the habits, ways, and customs of analogy-users.

1. In Frederick Jackson Turner, *The Frontier in American History* (1920; rpt. Tucson: University of Arizona Press, 1986), 2.

2. David M. Wrobel, *The End of American Exceptionalism: Frontier Anxiety from the Old West to the New Deal* (Lawrence: University Press of Kansas, 1993), 145.

3. Robert Cahn, "The Intrepid Kids of Disneyland," *Saturday Evening Post,* June 18, 1958, 22–23.

4. Ibid., 120.

5. Ibid., 119.

6. Ira Wolfert, "Walt Disney's Magic Kingdom," *Reader's Digest,* April 1960, 147.

7. Ibid., 147.

8. John M. Findlay, *Magic Lands: Western Cityscapes and American Culture after 1940* (Berkeley: University of California Press, 1992), 93–94.

9. Change seems to have been equally dramatic in Disney thinking about Indians. In 1993, the Walt Disney Company announced plans for a new American history theme park in Virginia. The section called "Native America," one company representative said, would now display "the sophisticated, intelligent societies that existed here before European settlers came, and in fact wiped out their societies" (Michael Wines, "Disney Will 'Recreate' U.S. History next to a Place Where It Was Made," *New York Times,* November 12, 1993).

10. See Patricia Nelson Limerick, Clyde A. Milner II, and Charles E. Rankin, eds., *Trails: Toward a New Western History* (Lawrence: University Press of Kansas, 1991).

11. Paula Petrik, *No Step Backward* (Helena: Montana Historical Society Press, 1987), chapter 2, "Capitalists with Rooms: Prostitution in Helena, 1865–1900," 25–58.

12. Historians have, of course, written on these topics, but they have sensibly avoided trying to package any of them as kinds of frontiers, parallel to the "mining frontier" or the "cattle frontier."

13. Jack D. Forbes, "Frontiers in American History," *Journal of the West* 1, nos. 1 and 2 (1962): 63–74, and "Frontiers in American History and the Role of the Frontier Historian," *Ethnohistory* 15 (Spring 1968): 203–35. I am quoting from the second, 207 and 205.

14. Howard Lamar and Leonard Thompson, eds., *The Frontier in History: North America and Southern Africa Compared* (New Haven, Conn.: Yale University Press, 1981), 7.

15. William Cronon, George Miles, and Jay Gitlin, "Becoming West: Toward a New Meaning for Western History," in *Under an Open Sky: Rethinking America's Western Past,* ed. Cronon, Miles, and Gitlin (New York: Norton, 1992), 3–27.

16. Stephen Aron, "Lessons in Conquest: Towards a Greater Western History," *Pacific Historical Review* 63 (May 1994).

17. Frank J. Popper, "The Strange Case of the Contemporary American Frontier," *The Yale Review* 76 (Autumn 1976), reprinted in *Major Problems in the History of the American West,* ed. Clyde Milner (Lexington, Mass.: Heath, 1989), 655.

18. Dayton Duncan, *Miles from Nowhere: Tales from America's Contemporary Frontier* (New York: Viking, 1993), 6–7.

19. Carl Abbott, *The Metropolitan Frontier: Cities in the Modern American West* (Tucson: University of Arizona Press, 1993). The definition of the frontier as a place of growth and opportunity is fairly common in urban history; see, for instance, Kenneth T. Jackson, *Crabgrass Frontier: The Suburbanization of the United States* (New York: Oxford University Press, 1985); and Joel Garreau, *Edge City: Life on the New Frontier* (New York: Doubleday, 1991).

20. Richard Bernstein, "Among Historians, the Old Frontier Is Turning Nastier with Each Revision," *New York Times,* December 17, 1989.

21. *"Let the Word Go Forth": The Speeches, Statements, and Writings of John F. Kennedy,* selected and with an introduction by Theodore C. Sorensen (New York: Delacorte Press, 1988), 100–102.

22. For a wide-ranging discussion of this assumption, see Wrobel, *The End of American Exceptionalism.*

23. *"Let the Word Go Forth,"* 100–102.

24. "President Very Much at Home on Ranch," *Denver Post,* August 23, 1986 (originally *Washington Post*).

25. United Press International, "Complete text of President Reagan's remarks," July 5, 1982.

26. "Transcript of Second Inaugural Address by Reagan," *New York Times,* January 22, 1985.

27. William Safire, "Grading the Speech," *New York Times,* January 24, 1985.

28. "Text of the President's State of the Union Address to Congress," *New York Times,* February 7, 1985.

29. Dukakis borrowed this phrase from Robert B. Reich's influential book, *The Last American Frontier: A Provocative Program for Economic Renewal* (1983; rpt. New York: Penguin, 1984). Reich himself subscribed to a modified "safety valve" image of the nineteenth-century frontier:

> During the years when the foundation of America's culture was being fixed, avoiding social conflict was far easier than settling it. The vastness of America's territories enabled generations of Americans to solve social problems by escaping from them, instead of working to change them. So long as the frontier beckoned, the sensible way to settle disputes was not painful negotiation, but simply putting some distance between the disputants. American notions of civic virtue came to center less on co-operating with neighbors than on leaving them alone. (p. 7)

30. "The Basic Speech/Michael Dukakis: A Call to Meet the Challenges of 'the Next American Frontier,'" *New York Times,* January 4, 1988.

31. Headlines are from the *Boulder Daily Camera* and the *Denver Post,* August 1986; the final one, "Frontier Legacy Lives," is from the *Denver Post,* August 5, 1991.

32. Molly O'Neill, "Eating to Heal: The New Frontiers," *New York Times,* February 7, 1990; "Edward Louie Is Dead, Cookie Pioneer was 69," Associated Press, May 31, 1990; "Two Cinnamon Roll Pioneers Are Spicing Up Product Line," *Nation's Restaurant News,* June 6, 1988; Cecilia Deck, "Fast-Food Pioneer A&W Survives to Map Comeback," *Chicago Tribune,* November 19, 1989; Berkley Hudson, "Laura Scudder Was More Than a Name; Monterey Park Will Honor 'Pioneer, Instigator, Doer' Who Helped Create Snack-Food Industry," *Los Angeles Times,* April 9, 1989; Marcia Dunn, "Pioneer in Natural Foods; Organic Farm Founder Had 50-Year Head Start," *Los Angeles Times,* January 15, 1989; Felicia Gressette, "Pioneer Vegetarian Fests Get '90s Update," *Miami Herald,* February 18, 1993; Judith Sims, "A Walk in the Garden with Pioneer of Edible Landscape," *Los Angeles Times,* February 25, 1989; Andrew Gumbel, "Pasta Pioneers," *Chicago Tribune,* December 15, 1988; "Potato Pioneer Dead at 73," United Press International, June 20,

1989; Russell Mitchell, "Golden Valley Needs a Side of Fries: A Pioneer in Microwave Popcorn," *Business Week,* November 7, 1988; Andy Wallace, "Antoinette Iannelli, Restaurateur and Pioneer of the South Philadelphia Hoagie," *Philadelphia Inquirer,* April 8, 1992.

33. Mary Rowland, "The Passionate Pioneer of Fitness Franchising," *Working Woman,* November 1988; Joe Ditler, "Surfing Pioneer Donald Takayama is Chairman of the Board Again," *Los Angeles Times,* May 3, 1990; Steve Morse, "A Psychedelic Pioneer Remembered," *Boston Globe,* June 16, 1989; Marianne Meyer, "New Age Pioneers," *Marketing and Media Decisions,* February 1988; Eric Lichtblau, "Sex-Change Pioneer Sues a Mission Viejo Hospital for Damages," *Los Angeles Times,* December 2, 1988, and "Sex-Change Pioneer Jorgensen," Associated Press, May 4, 1989; John Johnson and Michael Connelly, "A Porn Pioneer Still Baffles Police, Peers," *Los Angeles Times,* August 20, 1989; Pete Bowles, "A Drug 'Pioneer' Gets Life—Pioneer in the City's Crack Business," *Newsday,* December 2, 1989; Michael Kilian, "Frederick's: Peekaboo Pioneer," *Chicago Tribune,* June 6, 1990; "Underwear Pioneers Targeting Men," *Chicago Tribune,* December 24, 1989; Michael Arndt, "Amoco Spins a Reward for Polyester Pioneer," *Chicago Tribune,* May 4, 1989; "Inventor of Lexan®, Resin and Plastics Pioneer Dies," PR Newswire, February 17, 1989; Lisa Ann Casey, "Stainless Steel Cookware Pioneer," *Weekly Home Furnishings Newspaper,* April 17, 1989.

34. "Pioneer in Root Canal Dentistry," *Los Angeles Times,* March 29, 1988; David Hancock, "Sleeper-Sofa Pioneer Bernard Castro Dies," *Miami Herald,* August 25, 1991.

35. Roosevelt letter to Vannevar Bush, reprinted in Bush's *Science—the Endless Frontier: A Report to the President on a Program for Postwar Scientific Research* (Washington, D.C.: National Science Foundation, 1945; rpt. 1960), 3–4.

36. Ibid., 8.

37. *Pioneering the Space Frontier: The Report of the National Commission on Space* (New York: Bantam Books, 1986), 3–4. See also Gerard K. O'Neill, *The High Frontier: Human Colonies in Space* (Princeton, N.J.: Space Studies

Institute Press, 1989); and Harry L. Shipman, *Humans in Space: Twenty-first Century Frontiers* (New York: Plenum Press, 1989). Shipman's remark—"Americans, in particular, value exploration in and of itself because of the importance of the frontier in our history" (27)—typifies the space boosters' understanding of the history of westward expansion. For a more extensive discussion of the cultural psychology of the space program, see Patricia Nelson Limerick, "Imagined Frontiers: Westward Expansion and the Future of the Space Program," in *Space Policy Alternatives,* ed. Radford Byerly, Jr. (Boulder, Colo.: Westview, 1992).

38. See Oscar J. Martínez, *Troublesome Border* (Tucson: University of Arizona Press, 1986); Mario T. García, "La Frontera: The Border as Symbol and Reality in Mexican-American Thought," *Mexican Studies,* Summer 1985, 195–225; Alan Weisman and Jay Dusard, *La Frontera: The United States Border with Mexico* (Tucson: University of Arizona Press, 1986); Tom Miller, *On the Border: Portraits of America's Southwestern Frontier* (New York: Harper and Row, 1981).

39. Gloria Anzaldúa, *Borderlands/La Frontera: The New Mestiza* (San Francisco: Aunt Lute Books, 1987), 3.

40. Ibid., 4.

41. See Luis Alberto Urrea, *Across the Wire: Life and Hard Times on the Mexican Border* (New York: Doubleday, 1993).

42. Anzaldúa, *Borderlands/La Frontera,* 63.

43. "Thousands Form Human Chain across Romania-Bulgaria Frontier," Reuters, June 8, 1990; "Palestinian Guerrilla is Killed at Lebanese-Israeli Frontier," *New York Times,* September 6, 1989; "Algeria and Morocco Reopen their Frontier," Reuters, June 5, 1988; Jim Bodgener, "Turkey Will Close its Frontier with Bulgaria Today," *Financial Times,* August 22, 1989.

44. David Maraniss, "Memories in Black and White; Desegregation's Pioneers," *Washington Post,* June 6, 1990; "Genevieve Stuttaford Reviews *A. Philip Randolph: Pioneer of the Civil Rights Movement,*" *Publishers Weekly,* May 11, 1990; "Rights Pioneer Parks Hospitalized," *Los Angeles Times,* February 2, 1989; "City in Ohio Honors Civil Rights Pioneer," *Chicago Tribune,* May 11,

1990; Tanya Barrientos, "Civil Rights Pioneer Julian Bond Perplexed by Persistence of Racism," *Philadelphia Inquirer,* May 9, 1992; David Treadwell, "She is the First Black to Give Commencement Address: Integration Pioneer Returns to Speak at U. of Georgia," *Los Angeles Times,* June 12, 1988; "Thelma Cowans, Pioneer Black Professional Golfer, Dies," United Press International, February 7, 1990; Rosemary L. Bray, "Renaissance for a Pioneer of Black Pride," *New York Times,* February 4, 1990; G. D. Clay, "First, There Was Fritz; Long before Art Shell, Pollard was NFL's Pioneer Black Coach," *Newsday,* December 20, 1989; "Didi Daniels Peter; Pioneer Black Producer," *Los Angeles Times,* March 2, 1989; "Joseph W. Bostic: Pioneer Black Announcer," *Los Angeles Times,* June 2, 1988; Charles Fountain, "A Baseball Historian Goes to Bat for Some Negro League Greats: Blackball Stars: Negro League Pioneers," *Christian Science Monitor,* April 15, 1988; C. Gerald Fraser, "J. Saunders Redding, 81, Is Dead; Pioneer Black Ivy League Teacher," *New York Times,* March 5, 1988; David Mills, "Tuned In to Jockey Jack; Tribute to a Black Radio Pioneer," *Washington Post,* June 23, 1990; "Clifton R. Wharton Sr. Dies; Foreign Service Pioneer," *Jet,* May 14, 1990; "Pioneer Black L.A. Judge Edwin Jefferson Dies at 84," *Jet,* September 18, 1989; "Pioneer Black Journalist Albert J. Dunsmore, 73, Praised at Detroit Rites," *Jet,* February 20, 1989; Tia Swanson, "A Pioneer in World of Black Film," *Philadelphia Inquirer,* June 4, 1992; "Black Oscar Nominees Gala Celebrates Movie Talents (Sidney Poitier Wins Pioneer Award)," *Jet,* April 17, 1989; Gene Siskel, "Poitier the Pioneer: He's Back on Screen—and Taking a Second Look at a Life Full of Firsts," *Chicago Tribune,* January 31, 1988; Nick Jesdanun, "'Pioneer' Futures," *Newsday,* June 24, 1989.

45. "NL President Plays Down 'Pioneer' Talk," *Chicago Tribune,* May 16, 1989. See also "NL Boss Won't Wear Pioneer Tag," *USA Today,* May 16, 1989.

46. The first efforts at including African Americans within Western American history left the framework of traditional frontier history unchallenged. In the introduction to the first edition of *The Black West* (1971; rpt. Seattle, Wash.: Open Hand Publishing, 1987), William Loren Katz remarked, "When historian Frederick Jackson Turner told how the frontier shaped American democracy, he ignored the black experience—not because it

challenged his central thesis, but because he wrote in a tradition that had de-
nied the existence of black people" (xii). By the time of a later edition, Katz
was developing a more critical approach; consider this remark from the 1987
introduction:

A U.S. Army that treated its Buffalo Soldiers [African American men enlisted in the
post–Civil War western army] shabbily and cynically buried their military record,
has accepted an image rehabilitation and trumpeted black heroism the better to re-
cruit despairing, unemployed black youths. Will it, in the name of troopers who
battled Apaches, Sioux and Commanches, train dark young men to stem Third
World liberation forces? This would be a tragic misuse of the past. (xi)

See also William Leckie, *The Buffalo Soldiers* (Norman: University of Oklahoma Press, 1967). The recent issuing of a United States Post Office stamp
commemorating the Buffalo Soldiers puts an unintended spotlight on the
question of the African American role in conquest; see "Part of America's
Past Becomes a Stamp of Tomorrow," *New York Times,* December 8, 1993.

47. Don Terry, "A Graver Jackson's Cry: Overcome the Violence!" *New York
Times,* November 11, 1993.

48. Arthur Schlesinger, Jr., *The Disuniting of America: Reflections on a Multicultural
Society* (New York: Whittle Books, 1991).

49. These impressions come from a number of speaking engagements with
United States Information Agency tour groups, where international scholars
have told me about their early encounters with the American frontier myth.

CHECKLIST OF MATERIALS EXHIBITED

This list closely follows the narrative of the exhibition. Its arrangement is thematic rather than alphabetical, and the thematic headings have been revised to cater to readers rather than exhibition visitors. For books, the element exhibited is the cover when no plate or page number is given (in brackets, at the end of the entry). Reproductions in this book are cross-referenced at the appropriate entry.

Unless otherwise indicated, items listed are in the Newberry Library's collections. The exhibition includes items from the following Newberry special collections: the Edward E. Ayer Collection, the James Francis Driscoll Collection, and the George A. Poole III Collection. Current merchandise, vintage objects, and ephemera are not included in this checklist.

Introduction to Nineteenth-Century Images

Benson J. Lossing. *Our Country: A Household History for All Readers from the Discovery of America to the Present Time,* vol. 2. New York: Johnson and Miles, 1878. Everett D. Graff Collection. [Plate following page 1180]

FRONTISPIECE

"Murder of the whole Family of Samuel Wells, consisting of his wife and sister and eleven children, by the Indians: Extract of a letter from a gentleman in New Orleans, to his friend in New-York, dated May 1, 1809." Broadside [1813]. Edward E. Ayer Collection.

FIGURE 13

[G. A. Fleming]. *California: Its Past History, Its Present Position, Its Future Prospects.* London: The Proprietors, 1850. Everett D. Graff Collection. [Title page and frontispiece]

PLATE 1

"The Massacre of United States Troops by the Sioux and Cheyenne Indians Near Fort Philip Kearney, Dakotah Territory, December 22nd, 1866." Photograph of an etching in *Frank Leslie's Illustrated Newspaper* 23, no. 590 (January 19, 1876): 281.

A. Backus. "Tippecanoe Waltz." Sheet music. Troy, N.Y.: A. Backus, 1840. James Francis Driscoll Collection, box 162 (Whig folder).

George Caleb Bingham. *Daniel Boone Escorting Settlers through the Cumberland Gap.* Oil on canvas, 1851–52. Washington University Gallery of Art, St. Louis, Missouri. Gift of Nathaniel Phillips, 1890. Mural-sized photograph reproduced courtesy Washington University Gallery of Art.

FIGURE 2

Frederick Jackson Turner's Frontier

Frederick Jackson Turner. "The Significance of the Frontier in American History." *Annual Report of the American Historical Association for the Year 1893,* 197–227. Washington, D.C.: Government Printing Office, 1894.

Pictorial Map Showing the Route Travelled by the Mormon Pioneers from Nauvoo to Great Salt Lake. Salt Lake City: Millroy and Hayes, [1899]. Everett D. Graff Collection.

PLATE 2

Emma Willard. *A Series of Maps to Willard's History of the U.S.; or, Republic of America. Designed for Schools and Private Libraries.* Bound collection of maps. New York: White, Gallagher and White, 1828. [Eighth Map]

FIGURE 6

Guillaume de Lisle. *Carte de la Louisiane et du Cours du Mississipi.* Map. Paris, 1718.

FIGURE 5

Johann Christian Jaeger. *Schauplatz des Kriegs zwischen Engelland und seinen Collonien in America. . . .* Map. Frankfurt: J. C. Berndt, 1776.

Francis F. Palmer. *The Rocky Mountains—Emigrants Crossing the Plains.* Lithograph, 1866. Courtesy Chicago Historical Society.

Francis F. Palmer. *Across the Continent: "Westward the Course of Empire Takes Its Way."* Lithograph. New York: Currier and Ives, 1868. George A. Poole III Collection.

FIGURE 4

A. R. Waud. "Railroad Buildings on the Great Plains." Etching, *Harper's Weekly* 19, no. 968 (July 17, 1875): 577.

Colonel Frank Triplett. *Conquering the Wilderness; or, New Pictorial History of the Heros and Heroines of America. . . .* New York: N. D. Thompson, 1883. Everett D. Graff Collection. [Frontispiece]

FIGURE 3

Georges Henri Victor Collot. *Voyage dans l'Amérique septentrionale. . . .* Paris: Arthus Bertrand, 1826. Edward E. Ayer Collection. [Plate 16]

FIGURE 7

H. B. Pierce. *History of Calhoun County, Michigan.* Philadelphia: L. H. Everts and Co., 1877. [Page opposite 185]

FIGURE 10

Joseph Smith. *Old Redstone; or, Historical Sketches of Western Presbyterianism: Its Early Ministers, Its Perilous Times, and Its First Records.* Philadelphia: Lippencott, Grambo, 1854. [Photograph of page opposite 152]

FIGURE 9

Tippecanoe, the Hero of North Bend: Six Patriotic Ballads. . . . Sheet music. Composed by a Member of the Fifth Ward Club. New York: Thomas Birch, 1840. James Francis Driscoll Collection, box 162 (Whig folder).

FIGURE 8

Chicago in Early Days: 1779–1857. Lithograph. Chicago: Louis Kurz and Alexander Allison, 1893. Poster reproduction, 1974, Historic Urban Plans, Ithaca, New York, from an original in its collections.

A. T. Andreas. *History of Chicago from the Earliest Period to the Present Time,* vol. 1. Chicago: A. T. Andreas, 1884. Edward E. Ayer Collection. [Reproduction of frontispiece]

FIGURE 23

George Davis. *Chicago in 1832.* Poster. "Tribute to the World's Columbian Exposition." Chicago: Rufus Blanchard, n.d. [ca. 1893]. George A. Poole III Collection.

FIGURE 11

Atlas of Franklin County, Indiana. Chicago: J. H. Beers and Co., 1882. [Pages 64 and 65]

Biographical History of Shelby and Audubon Counties, Iowa. Chicago: W. S. Dunbar, 1889. [Title page and annotated flyleaf]

A. J. Turner. *The Family Tree of Columbia County, Wis[consin].* Columbia County Board of Supervisors, 1904. [First illustration reproduced; photograph courtesy State Historical Society of Wisconsin.]

FIGURE 22

Portrait and Biographical Record of St. Clair County, Illinois. Chicago: Chapman Bros., 1892. [Page opposite 522]

Frederick Jackson Turner. "The Stream of Immigration into the United States." *Chicago Record Herald,* September 25, 1901.

Collage of turn-of-the-century Chicago immigrant photographs. Photographs courtesy Prints and Photographs Department, Chicago Historical Society (photograph nos. ICHI 02524, BC 201, ICHI 25036, BC 202, ICHI 25194, ICHI 02027, ICHI 03808).

Buffalo Bill Cody's Wild West

Vince Dillon. "These Boys Found the 101 Wild Ranch Wild West Show Couriers Exciting Reading." Undated photograph, courtesy Western History Collections, University of Oklahoma Libraries.

Advertisement for Buffalo Bill's Wild West. *Chicago Daily News,* April 27, 1893.

Buffalo Bill's Wild West and Congress of Rough Riders of the World: Historical Sketches and Programme. Chicago: Blakely Printing Company, 1893. Everett D. Graff Collection.

FIGURE 1

D. Emerson. *Galop for the Piano.* Sheet music. New York: William H. Pond and Co., 1888. James Francis Driscoll Collection, box 162 (West folder).

John M. Burke. *Buffalo Bill: From Prairie to Palace.* Chicago: Rand McNally and Co., 1839. Everett D. Graff Collection.

William F. Cody. *Story of the Wild West and Camp-Fire Chats.* Philadelphia: Historical Publication Co., 1888. Edward E. Ayer Collection. [Title page and frontispiece]

PLATE 5

Congress of American Indians. Poster for Buffalo Bill's Wild West. Buffalo, New York: Printed by Courier Lithographic Co., 1899. Photograph courtesy Library of Congress.

Buffalo Bill's Wild West. Poster for Buffalo Bill's Wild West. Paris: Printed by Chaix, 1905. Photograph courtesy Buffalo Bill Historical Center, Cody, Wyoming.

On the Stage Coach. Poster for Buffalo Bill's Wild West. Color Lithograph. Baltimore, Maryland: Printed by Hoen & Co., 1893. Gift of the Coe Foundation. Photograph courtesy Buffalo Bill Museum, Cody, Wyoming.

Mary Rowlandson. *A Narrative of the Captivity, Suffering, and Removes of Mrs. Mary Rowlandson who was taken prisoner by the Indians. . . .* Boston: N. Covery, 1771. Edward E. Ayer Collection. [Title page]

Thomas Baldwin. *Narrative of the Massacre, by the Savages, of the Wife and Children of Thomas Baldwin.* New York: Martin's Wood, 1835. Edward E. Ayer Collection. [Title page and frontispiece]

Henry Howe. *The Great West: The Vast, Illimitable, Changing West.* New York: George F. Tuttle, 1860. [Page opposite 157]

FIGURE 14

George Armstrong Custer. *Wild Life on the Plains.* St. Louis, Missouri: Royal Publishing Co., 1891. Edward E. Ayer Collection. [Plate following contents page]

FIGURE 18

T. M. Newson. *Thrilling Scenes among the Indians with a Graphic Description of Custer's Last Fight with Sitting Bull.* Chicago: Belford Clarke and Co., 1884. Everett D. Graff Collection. [Page opposite 189]

Frederick Whittaker. *A Complete Life of Major Gen'l George A. Custer: Major-General of Volunteers, Brevet Major-General U.S. Army, and Lieutenant-Colonel Seventh U.S. Cavalry.* New York: Sheldon and Co., 1876.

Three undated postcards. Elmo Scott Watson Collection, box 6 (Custer Battle Paintings folder), Edward E. Ayer Collection. Postcards titled as follows:

"General Custer's Last Charge"
"Custer's Last Fight"
"Custer's Last Fight from Old Print"

Charles Clover. *Requiem to the Memory of Gen. Geo. A. Custer.* Sheet music. New York: William H. Pond and Co., 1876. James Francis Driscoll Collection, box 162 (Whig folder).

"Custer's Tragic Battlefield where on June 25th, 1876 the Gallant Major General and his Little Band of Men were Overwhelmed and Killed by Warriors of the Sioux and Cheyenne Tribes. . . ." Undated postcard. Elmo Scott Watson Collection, box 6 (Custer Battlefield folder), Edward E. Ayer Collection.

"Semi-Centennial of the Battle of the Little Big Horn Custer's Last Stand: On the Battlefield—Crow Agency, Mont., June 24, 25, 26, 1926." Undated pamphlet issued by P. S. Eustis, Passenger Traffic Manager, Chicago. Elmo Scott Watson Collection, box 6 (Custer Battlefield folder), Edward E. Ayer Collection.

J. W. Buel. *Heroes of the Plains; or, Life and Wonderful Adventures of Wild Bill, Buffalo Bill and Exploits. . . .* St. Louis, Missouri: N. D. Thompson, 1881. Everett D. Graff Collection. [Page opposite 396]

PLATE 3

"Sitting Bull and Buffalo Bill." Undated postcard. Elmo Scott Watson Collection, box 15 (Sitting Bull, Tatanka i-Yotanka, Hunk papa Sioux folder), Edward E. Ayer Collection.

FIGURE 12

Colonel Prentiss Ingraham. *Buffalo Bill with General Custer; or, Friends to the End.* New York: Street and Smith, 1914.

PLATE 4

"Custer's Last Fight." Poster advertisement, first edition. Lithographic print. St. Louis, Missouri: Anheuser-Busch Brewing Association, 1896. Courtesy Anheuser-Busch Corporate Archives.

FIGURE 15

Program for Buffalo Bill and Captain Jack, in *Life on the Border,* Oakland, California, June 13, 1877. San Francisco: Printed by Francis Valentine, 1877. Everett D. Graff Collection. [Cover, front and back]

FIGURE 16

"Capt. Jack Crawford, Poet-Scout of the Black Hills." Undated postcard. Elmo Scott Watson Collection, box 10 (Crawford, Capt. Jack folder), Edward E. Ayer Collection.

"Ladies Night: An Evening with Brother Capt. Jack Crawford." Ticket, April 16, 1910. Elmo Scott Watson Collection, box 10 (Crawford, Capt. Jack folder), Edward E. Ayer Collection.

Captain Jack Crawford. *The Poet Scout: A Book of Song and Story.* New York: Funk and Wagnalls, 1886. Edward E. Ayer Collection.

FIGURE 17

Alfred Sorenson. Typed, signed letter to Elmo Scott Watson, May 23, 1938. Elmo Scott Watson Collection, box 10 (Crawford, Capt. Jack folder), Edward E. Ayer Collection.

Captain Jack Crawford. *Little Ones Praying at Home.* Sheet music. Boston: Louis H. Ross and Co., 1888. James Francis Driscoll Collection, box 162 (West folder).

Lakota and Cheyenne Stories

"Cheyenne Ledger Book." Undated. Edward E. Ayer Collection. [Pages 6, 7, 22]

FIGURE 19

Amos Bad Heart Buffalo. Four paintings reproduced in *Sioux Indian Painting: The Art of Amos Bad Heart Buffalo, with Introduction and Notes by Hartley Burr Alexander*. Part 2. Nice: C. Szwedzicki, 1938. Edward E. Ayer Collection. The notes for each painting begin as follows:

plate 2, "Opening of the Battle of the Little Big Horn . . ."
plate 7, "Last moments of the encounter with General Custer's Troops . . ."

PLATE 6

plate 13, "Troopers being driven across the river . . ."
plate 17, "A colored drawing by Amos Bad Heart Buffalo of the last moments of the encounter with General Custer's Troops."

Hogan'-Lu'Ta (Red Fish). Undated painting on paper with an annotation, "Custer as a White Man," attributed to Aaron McGaffey Beede. Fort Yates Collection, plate 151. Edward E. Ayer Collection.

Hogan'-Lu'Ta (Red Fish). Undated painting on cardboard with an annotation, "Custer as a Comanche . . . ," on the back attributed to Aaron McGaffey Beede. Fort Yates Collection, plate 152. Edward E. Ayer Collection.

PLATE 7

[No-Two-Horn]. "This shows S. Bull by Custer's dead body about sunset. . . ." [Title/annotation attributed to Aaron McGaffey Beede, who commissioned the work.] Undated painting opposite title page in a copy of Beede's *Sitting Bull– Custer* (Bismarck, N.D.: Bismarck Tribune Company, 1913). From a complete photostatic reproduction of the book. Edward E. Ayer Collection (location of original painted edition unknown).

[No-Two-Horn]. "This shows S. Bull by Custer's dead body about sunset. . . ." [Title/annotation attributed to Aaron McGaffey Beede, who commissioned the work.] Hand-colored photograph of painting opposite title page in a copy of Beede's *Sitting Bull–Custer*. Edward E. Ayer Collection, box 1 (location of original painting unknown).

FIGURE 20

Hamlin Garland. "General Custer's Last Fight As Seen by Two Moon: The Battle Described by a Chief Who Took Part in It." *McClure's Magazine* 11, no. 5 (September 1898): 441–48.

Elbridge Ayer Burbank. *Rain-in-the-Face. Sioux.* Oil on board, 1898. Signed "E. A. Burbank, Rock Cree S[outh] D[akota], 1898." Burbank Oil Portrait Collection, no. 76, Edward E. Ayer Collection.

FIGURE 21

Elbridge Ayer Burbank. *Chief American Horse. Northern Cheyenne.* Oil on canvas. Signed "E. A. Burbank, Lame Deer, Mont., 1897." Burbank Oil Portrait Collection, no. 72, Edward E. Ayer Collection.

Alma M. Lorenz. "Custer's Last Battle in New Light: Sioux Indians Come Forward with Claims to Fortify Their Contention That What American Schoolbooks Term a Massacre in the Black Hills was a Battle Fairly Fought. . . ." Undated clipping, source unknown. Elmo Scott Watson Collection, box 6 (Indian Accounts folder), Edward E. Ayer Collection.

Cowboys

Three Riders. Poster for Buffalo Bill's Wild West. Paris: Printed by Chaix, 1905. Photograph courtesy Circus World Museum, Baraboo, Wisconsin.

Buffalo Bill's Wild West and Congress of Rough Riders of the World: Actual Scenes, Genuine Characters. Poster for Buffalo Bill's Wild West. Buffalo, N.Y.: Printed by Courier Co., 1896. Photograph courtesy Circus World Museum, Baraboo, Wisconsin.

Annie Oakley. Poster for Buffalo Bill's Wild West. Cincinnati, Ohio: Enquirer Job Printing Co., 1901. Photograph courtesy Circus World Museum, Baraboo, Wisconsin.

Annie Oakley/Johnnie Baker. Poster in three sheets for Buffalo Bill's Wild West. Cincinnati, Ohio: Enquirer Job Printing Co., 1898. Photograph courtesy Circus World Museum, Baraboo, Wisconsin.

Wallace Smith. *Let'er Buck.* Undated. Miniaturized reproduction of a poster printed by West Coast Engraving Co., Oregon. Elmo Scott Watson Collection, box 8 (Western Painters folder), Edward E. Ayer Collection.

Charles Siringo. *A Texas Cow Boy; or, Fifteen Years on the Hurricane Deck of a Spanish Pony.* Chicago: Siringo and Dobsen, 1886. Everett D. Graff Collection. [Frontispiece]

PLATE 8

Bob Grantham Quickfall. *Western Life and How I Became a Bronco Buster: Founded on Facts.* London: F. Charles and Co., [1891?]. Everett D. Graff Collection.

Theodore Roosevelt. *Ranch Life and the Hunting Trail.* New York: Century Co., 1901. Edward E. Ayer Collection.

Frederic Remington. *Drawings by Frederic Remington.* Edited by Owen Wister. New York: Robert Howard Russell, 1897. Everett D. Graff Collection. [Plate titled "A 'Sun Fisher'"]

To the Rescue. Poster for Buffalo Bill's Wild West. Baltimore, Maryland. Printed by Hoen & Co., 1894. Courtesy Buffalo Bill Museum, Cody, Wyoming.

FIGURE 24

Eduard Holst. *The Charge of the Rough Riders: Grand Galop Militaire.* Sheet music. New York: Howley, Haviland and Co., 1898. James Francis Driscoll Collection, box 158 (Theodore Roosevelt folder).

FIGURE 25

Frederic Remington. *The Bronco Buster.* Bronze cast. Photograph courtesy Buffalo Bill Museum, Cody, Wyoming.

Theodore Roosevelt. Western Union telegram to Frederic Remington, September 19, 1898. Photograph courtesy Frederic Remington Art Museum, Ogdensburg, New York.

Charles M. Russell. *The Old Story.* Watercolor, signed and dated 1910. Photograph courtesy C. M. Russell Museum, Great Falls, Montana.

Charles M. Russell. Signed and illustrated autograph letter to "Friend Trigg," February 24, 1916. Photograph courtesy C. M. Russell Museum, Great Falls, Montana.

Charles M. Russell. Signed and illustrated autograph letter to "Friend Bob [Thoroughman]," April 14, 1920. Photograph courtesy C. M. Russell Museum, Great Falls, Montana.

Charles M. Russell. "The West Is Dead My Friend." Original, signed, drawing and verse inscribed in a copy of Frank Bird Linderman's *Indian Why Stories; Sparks from War Eagle's Lodge-fire.* 1917. Photograph courtesy C. M. Russell Museum, Great Falls, Montana.

The Farewell Shot. Poster for Buffalo Bill's Wild West. Cincinnati, Ohio, 1910. Photograph courtesy Buffalo Bill Historical Center, Cody, Wyoming.

Death and Rebirth of the American Frontier

Advertisement for the Jordan automobile. *Saturday Evening Post,* July 23, 1923. Photograph courtesy Seattle Public Library.

PLATE 9

Florence Ryerson. "The Codfish Princess." *Sunset* 41 (September 1918): 41–43.

Advertisement for the motion picture *Renegades. Life,* April 15, 1946.

Major Horace Bell. *Reminiscences of a Ranger.* Santa Barbara, California: Wallace Hebbard, 1927. [Page opposite 153]

Clason's Touring Atlas of the United States and Canada. Chicago: Clason Map Co., [1920].

PLATE 10

Illinois Highway Guide: Official 1931 Edition. State of Illinois Automobile Department. From the private collection of James R. Akerman.

Ohio 1938 Official Highway Map. Revised to February 15, 1938. State of Ohio Department of Highways. From the private collection of James R. Akerman. [Cover]

1940 Arizona Road Map. Arizona State Highway Department. Map archives.

Telling the Stories Anew

Kenneth Libo and Irving Howe. *We Lived Here Too: In Their Own Words and Pictures—Pioneer Jews and the Westward Movement of America, 1630–1930*. New York: St. Martin's/Marek, 1984.

Mario T. García. *Desert Immigrants: The Mexicans of El Paso, 1880–1920*. Yale Western American Series, no. 32. New Haven, Connecticut: Yale University Press, 1981.

Julie Roy Jeffrey. *Frontier Women: The Trans Mississippi West, 1846–1880*. American Century Series. New York: Hill and Wang, 1979.

Daniel H. Usner, Jr. *Indians, Settlers, and Slaves in a Frontier Exchange Economy: The Lower Mississippi Valley Before 1783*. Chapel Hill: University of North Carolina Press, 1992.

Ramón A. Gutiérrez. *When Jesus Came, the Corn Mothers Went Away: Marriage, Sexuality, and Power in New Mexico, 1500–1846*. Stanford, California: Stanford University Press, 1991.

Francis Casimir Kajencki. *Poles in the Nineteenth Century Southwest*. El Paso, Texas: Southwest Polonia Press, 1990.

Nell Irvin Painter. *Exodusters: Black Migration to Kansas after Reconstruction*. New York: Knopf, 1977.